EYEWITNESS TRAVEL GUIDES

GERMAN PHRASE BOOK

A Dorling Kindersley Book

LONDON, NEW YORK, MUNICH,
MELBOURNE, AND DELHI

Compiled by Lexus Ltd with Chris Stephenson and Horst Kopleck

First published in Great Britain in 1997
by Dorling Kindersley Limited
80 Strand, London WC2R 0RL

Reprinted with corrections 2000, 2003
4 6 8 10 9 7 5

A CIP catalogue record is available from the British Library.

ISBN 0 7513 6989 6

Printed and bound in China by Leo Paper Products Limited

Picture Credits
Jacket: Getty Images/Rin Chapple (centre);
Pinkus Muller Brewery (bottom left)

CONTENTS

PREFACE

This *Dorling Kindersley Eyewitness Travel Guides Phrase Book* has been compiled by experts to meet the general needs of tourists and business travellers. Arranged under headings such as Hotels, Driving and so forth, the ample selection of useful words and phrases is supported by a 2,000-line mini-dictionary. There is also an extensive menu guide listing approximately 600 dishes or methods of cooking and presentation.

Typical replies to questions you may ask during your journey, and the signs or instructions you may see or hear, are shown in tinted boxes. In the main text, the pronunciation of German words and phrases is imitated in English sound syllables. The Introduction provides guidelines to German pronunciation.

Dorling Kindersley Eyewitness Travel Guides are recognized as the world's best travel guides. Each title features specially commissioned colour photographs, detailed maps, cutaways of major buildings and 3-D aerial views, plus information on sights, events, hotels, restaurants, shopping and entertainment.

INTRODUCTION

Pronunciation

When reading the imitated pronunciation, stress the part that is underlined. Pronounce each syllable as if it formed part of an English word, and you will be understood sufficiently well. Remember the points below, and your pronunciation will be even closer to the correct German.

g is pronounced hard as in 'get'.

KH represents the guttural German 'ch' and should sound like the Scottish 'loch' (which <u>isn't</u> 'lock').

oo represents the long German 'u'; make this an English 'oo' as in 'food' (*not* short as in 'foot').

oo represents the shorter German 'u', as in English 'took', 'book'.

ꝏ is how we imitate the German 'ü', which sounds like the 'ee' in 'seen' if you pronounce it with rounded lips (or like the French 'u').

ow should sound like the 'ow' in 'cow' (*not* as in 'low').

'You' and 'I'

In most cases we have given the polite form for 'you' – which is **Sie** (*zee*). The familiar form **du** (*doo*) can also be used, but normally only if you are talking to someone you know well and would regard as a personal friend.

Questions involving 'I' have sometimes been translated with **man**, for example 'Can I ...?' **Kann man ...?**. Literally **man** means 'one' but is not a formal word as it is in English.

USEFUL EVERYDAY PHRASES

YES, NO, OK ETC

Yes/No
Ja/Nein
ya/nine

Good
Gut
goot

Excellent!
Ausgezeichnet!
owss-geh-tsysh-net

OK
Okay
okay

That's fine
In Ordnung
in ortnoong

That's right
Stimmt
shtimmt

GREETINGS, INTRODUCTIONS

How do you do, pleased to meet you
Guten Tag, freut mich
gooten tahk froyt mich

Good morning/good afternoon/good evening
Guten Morgen/Guten Tag/Guten Abend
gooten morgen/gooten tahk/gooten ahbent

Good night *(going to bed)*
Gute Nacht
gootuh nakht

(leaving late at night)
Auf Wiedersehen
owf veeder-zayn

Goodbye
Auf Wiedersehen
owf veeder-zayn

How are you?
Wie geht es Ihnen?
vee gayt ess eenen

(familiar form)
Wie geht es dir?
vee gayt ess deer

My name's …
Ich heiße …
ish hice-uh

What's your name?
Wie heißen Sie?
vee hice-en zee

(familiar form)
Wie heißt du?
vee hice-t doo

What's his/her name?
Wie heißt er/sie?
vee hice-t air/zee

May I introduce …?
Darf ich Ihnen … vorstellen?
darf ish eenen … for-shtellen

This is …
Das ist …
dass ist

Hello/Hi
Hallo
hallo

Bye!/Cheerio!
Tschüs!
chooss

See you later
Bis später
biss shpayter

It's been nice meeting you
Es war nett, Sie kennenzulernen
ess var nett zee kennen-tsoo-lairnen

Please, Thank You, Apologies

Thank you
Danke
dankuh

No, thank you
Nein, danke
nine dankuh

Please
Bitte
bittuh

Excuse me!
Entschuldigung!
ent-shooldigoong

Sorry!
Entschuldigung!
ent-shooldigoong

I'm really sorry
Tut mir wirklich leid
toot meer veerklish lite

It was my fault/it wasn't my fault
Es war meine Schuld/Es war nicht meine Schuld
ess var mine-uh shoolt/ess var nisht mine-uh shoolt

Where, How, Asking

Excuse me, please
Entschuldigen Sie bitte
ent-shooldigen zee bittuh

Can you tell me …?
Können Sie mir sagen …?
kurnen zee meer zahgen

Can I have …?
Kann ich … haben?
kan ish … hahben

Would you like a …?
Möchten Sie einen/eine/ein …?
murshten zee ine-en/ine-uh/ine

Would you like to …?
Möchten Sie …?
murshten zee

Is there … here?
Gibt es hier …?
geept ess heer

What's that?
Was ist das?
vass ist dass

Where can I get …?
Wo bekomme ich …?
vo bukommuh ish

How much is it?
Was kostet das?
vass kostet dass

Where is the …?
Wo ist der/die/das …?
vo ist dair/dee/dass

Is there wheelchair access?
Kann man dort mit einem Rollstuhl hinein?
kan man dohrt mit ine-nem rollstuhl hin-ine

Are there facilities for the disabled?
Sind die Einrichtungen behindertengerecht?
zint dee ine-rishtungen behindairtengeraisht

Are guide dogs allowed?
Sind Blindenhunde erlaubt?
zint blindenhoonduh airlowpt

About Oneself

I'm from …
Ich bin aus …
ish bin owss

I'm … years old
Ich bin … Jahre alt
ish bin … yaruh allt

I'm a …
Ich bin …
ish bin

I'm married/single/divorced
Ich bin verheiratet/single/geschieden
ish bin fairhyrahtet/single/gusheeden

I have … sisters/brothers/children
Ich habe … Schwestern/Brüder/Kinder
ish hahbuh … shvestern/brooder/kinder

Likes, Dislikes, Socialising

I like …
Ich möchte … gern
ish murshtuh … gairn

I love ...
Ich liebe ...
ish leebuh ...

I like swimming/travelling
Ich schwimme/reise gern
ish shvimmuh/ryzuh gairn

I don't like ...
Ich möchte ... nicht gern
ish murshtuh ... nisht gairn

I don't like swimming/travelling
Ich schwimme/reise nicht gern
ish shvimmuh/ryzuh nisht gairn

I hate ...
Ich hasse ...
ish hassuh

Do you like ...?
Möchten Sie ...?
murshten zee

It's delicious/awful!
Es ist köstlich/furchtbar!
ess ist kurstlish/foorshtbar

I don't drink/smoke
Ich trinke/rauche nicht
ish trinkuh/rowKHuh nisht

Do you mind if I smoke?
Haben Sie etwas dagegen, wenn ich rauche?
hahben zee etvass dagaygen ven ish rowKHuh

I don't eat meat or fish
Ich esse kein Fleisch und keinen Fisch
ish essuh kine flysh oont kine-en fish

What would you like (to drink)?
Was möchten Sie (trinken)?
vass murshten zee (trinken)

I would like a …
Ich möchte gern einen/eine/ein …
ish murshtuh gairn ine-en/ine-uh/ine

Nothing for me, thanks
Nichts für mich, danke
nishts fωr mish dankuh

I'll get this one
Das geht auf meine Rechnung
dass gayt owf mine-uh reshnoong

Cheers!
Prost!
prohst

I would like to …
Ich möchte gern …
ish murshtuh gairn

Let's go to Stuttgart/go to the cinema
Sollen wir nach Stuttgart fahren/ins Kino gehen?
zollen veer nahKH shtootgart faren/inss keeno gay-en

Let's go swimming/for a walk
Sollen wir schwimmen/spazieren gehen?
zollen veer shvimmen/shpatseeren gay-en

What's the weather like?
Wie ist das Wetter?
vee ist dass vetter

The weather's awful
Das Wetter ist furchtbar
dass vetter ist foorshtbar

It's pouring down
Es gießt
ess geest

It's really hot/sunny
Es ist wirklich heiß/sonnig
ess ist veerklish hice/zonnish

HELP, PROBLEMS (*see also* EMERGENCIES *p108*)

Can you help me?
Können Sie mir helfen?
kurnen zee meer helfen

I don't understand
Ich verstehe nicht
ish fairshtayuh nisht

Do you speak English/French?
Sprechen Sie Englisch/Französisch?
shpreshen zee eng-lish/frantsur-zish

Does anyone here speak English?
Spricht hier jemand Englisch?
shprisht heer yaymant eng-lish

I can't speak German
Ich spreche kein Deutsch
ish shpreshuh kine doytsh

I don't know
Ich weiß nicht
ish vice nisht

What's wrong?
Stimmt etwas nicht?
shtimmt etvass nisht

Please speak more slowly
Sprechen Sie bitte etwas langsamer
shpreshen zee bittuh etvass langzahmer

Please write it down for me
Könnten Sie es mir bitte aufschreiben?
kurnten zee ess meer bittuh owf-shryben

I've lost my way
Ich habe mich verlaufen
ish hahbuh mish fairlowfen

(driving)
Ich habe mich verfahren
ish hahbuh mish fairfaren

Where is the British Embassy?
Wo finde ich die Britische Botschaft?
voh finduh ish dee britishuh bohtshaft?

TALKING TO RECEPTIONISTS ETC

I have an appointment with …
Ich habe eine Verabredung mit …
ish hahbuh ine-uh fairap-raydoong mit

I'd like to see …
Ich möchte gern … sprechen
ish murshtuh gairn … shpreshen

Here's my card
Hier ist meine Karte
heer ist mine-uh kartuh

My company is …
Meine Firma ist …
mine-uh feerma ist

May I use the phone/photocopier/fax machine?
Kann ich das Telefon/das Fotokopiergerät/das Faxgerät benutzen?
kan ish dass telefohn/dass fotokopeargerayt/dass faxgerayt bunootsen

Things You'll Hear

Achtung!	attention, look out!
bedienen Sie sich	help yourself
bis später	see you later
bitte?	pardon?
bitte (schön/sehr)	here you are, you're welcome
bitte (schön/sehr)?	what is it? can I help you?
danke gleichfalls	the same to you
Entschuldigung	excuse me
genau	exactly
gut	good
guten Tag, freut mich	how do you do, nice to meet you
gute Reise	have a good trip
ich verstehe nicht	I don't understand
ich weiß nicht	I don't know
schöne Grüße an …	give my regards to …
stimmt	that's right
Verzeihung	excuse me
vielen Dank	thank you very much
wie bitte?	what did you say?
wie geht es Ihnen?	how are you?
wie geht's?	how are things?
wirklich?	is that so? really?

Things You'll See

Abfall	litter
Aufzug	lift
außer	except
außer Betrieb	out of order
Ausgang	way out, exit

→

Auskunft	information
belegt	no vacancies
besetzt	engaged
Besuchszeiten	visiting hours
bitte nicht …	please do not …
Damen	women
drücken	push
Eingang	way in, entrance
Eintritt	entry
Eintritt frei	admission free
Erdgeschoß	ground floor
Feiertag	public holiday
frisch gestrichen	wet paint
Fußgänger	pedestrians
Gefahr	danger
geöffnet	open
geschlossen	closed
Herren	men
kein(e) …	no …
kein Zutritt	no admittance
nicht …	do not …
Nichtraucher	no smoking
Notausgang	emergency exit
nur …	only …
Öffnungszeiten	opening times
Raucher	smokers
Straße	street
Stock	floor, storey
Tiefgeschoß	basement
untersagt	prohibited
verboten	forbidden
Vorsicht	take care
ziehen	pull
Zoll	customs
zu verkaufen	for sale
zu vermieten	for rent, for hire

COLLOQUIALISMS

You may hear these: to use some of them yourself could be risky!

alles klar!	fine, great
Arschloch	bastard
bekloppt	crazy
bescheuert	crazy, daft
besoffen	pissed, smashed
Blödsinn	nonsense, rubbish
doof	stupid
du lieber Gott!	good God!
du spinnst wohl!	you've got to be joking!, you're out of your mind!
Kumpel	pal
Mann!	boy!
Mensch!	wow!
nee	nope
Ossi	East German
sauer	pissed off
Schnauze!	shut your mouth!
Schwachkopf	idiot, wally
Schwachsinn	rubbish
Sonntagsfahrer!	Sunday driver!
Spitze	fantastic, magic
stark	great
super	great
toll!	tremendous!, brilliant!
Typ	guy, bloke
Unverschämtheit	cheek, nerve
verdammt noch mal!	bloody hell!
Wahnsinn!	fantastic!
Wessi	West German

DAYS, MONTHS, SEASONS

Sunday	Sonntag	*zontahk*
Monday	Montag	*mohntahk*
Tuesday	Dienstag	*deenstahk*
Wednesday	Mittwoch	*mitvoKH*
Thursday	Donnerstag	*donnerstahk*
Friday	Freitag	*frytahk*
Saturday	Samstag, Sonnabend	*zamstahk, zonnahbent*
January	Januar	*yanooar*
February	Februar	*faybrooar*
March	März	*mairts*
April	April	*april*
May	Mai	*my*
June	Juni	*yoonee*
July	Juli	*yoolee*
August	August	*owgoost*
September	September	*zeptember*
October	Oktober	*oktober*
November	November	*november*
December	Dezember	*daytsember*
Spring	Frühling	*frooling*
Summer	Sommer	*zommer*
Autumn	Herbst	*hairpst*
Winter	Winter	*vinter*
Christmas	Weihnachten	*vynaKHten*
Christmas Eve	Heiligabend	*hylish-ahbent*
New Year	Neujahr	*noy-yar*
New Year's Eve	Silvester	*zilvester*
Easter	Ostern	*ohstern*
Good Friday	Karfreitag	*karfrytahk*
Whitsun	Pfingsten	*pfingsten*

NUMBERS

0 null *nool*
1 eins *ine-ss*
2 zwei *tsvy*
3 drei *dry*
4 vier *feer*
5 fünf *foonf*
6 sechs *zex*
7 sieben *zeeben*
8 acht *aKHt*
9 neun *noyn*
10 zehn *tsayn*
11 elf *elf*
12 zwölf *tsvurlf*
13 dreizehn *dry-tsayn*
14 vierzehn *veer-tsayn*
15 fünfzehn *foonf-tsayn*
16 sechzehn *zesh-tsayn*
17 siebzehn *zeep-tsayn*
18 achtzehn *aKHt-tsayn*
19 neunzehn *noyn-tsayn*

20 zwanzig *tsvantsish*
21 einundzwanzig *ine-oont-tsvantsish*
22 zweiundzwanzig *tsvy-oont-tsvantsish*
30 dreißig *drysish*
40 vierzig *feertsish*
50 fünfzig *foonftsish*
60 sechzig *zeshtsish*
70 siebzig *zeeptsish*
80 achtzig *aKHtsish*
90 neunzig *noyntsish*
100 hundert *hoondert*
110 hundertzehn *hoondert-tsayn*
200 zweihundert *tsvy-hoondert*
1,000 tausend *towzent*
10,000 zehntausend *tsayn-towzent*
100,000 hunderttausend *hoondert-towzent*
1,000,000 eine Million *ine-uh mill-yohn*

Ordinal numbers are formed by adding **-te**, or **-ste** if the number ends in **-ig**. For example, **fünfte** (*foonftuh*, 'fifth'), **zwanzigste** (*tsvantsishstuh*, 'twentieth'). Exceptions are: **erste** (*airstuh*, 'first'), **dritte** (*drittuh*, 'third') and **siebte** (*zeeptuh*, 'seventh').

TIME

Telling the Time

To say the hour in German use the word **Uhr** (*oor*) preceded by the appropriate number, for example: **neun Uhr** (*noyn oor*) is 'nine o'clock'. The 24-hour clock is used much more commonly in Germany.

The word for 'past' is **nach** (*nahKH*). So **zehn nach neun** (*tsayn nahKH noyn*) is 'ten past nine'. The word for 'to' is **vor** (*for*). So **zehn vor neun** (*tsayn for noyn*) is 'ten to nine'. The word for '(a) quarter' is **viertel** (*feertel*). So **viertel nach/vor neun** (*feertel nahKH/for noyn*) is '(a) quarter past/to nine'.

The important thing to remember when telling the time is that, when talking about the half hour, Germans count back from the next full hour, so that, for example, 'half past nine' is said in German as 'half ten'. So **es ist halb zehn** (*ess ist halp tsayn*) means 'it's half past nine'. Think 'half to' instead of 'half past'.

Useful Words and Phrases

today	heute	*hoytuh*
yesterday	gestern	*gestern*
tomorrow	morgen	*morgen*
the day before yesterday	vorgestern	*forgestern*
the day after tomorrow	übermorgen	*oobermorgen*
this week	diese Woche	*deezuh voKHuh*
last week	letzte Woche	*letstuh voKHuh*
next week	nächste Woche	*naykstuh voKHuh*
this morning	heute morgen	*hoytuh morgen*
this afternoon	heute nachmittag	*hoytuh nahKHmit-tahk*
this evening	heute abend	*hoytuh ahbent*
tonight	heute abend	*hoytuh ahbent*

yesterday afternoon	gestern nachmittag	*gestern nahKHmit-tahk*
last night		
(last evening)	gestern Abend	*gestern ahbent*
(late at night)	gestern Nacht	*gestern naKHt*
tomorrow morning	morgen früh	*morgen froo*
tomorrow night	morgen abend	*morgen ahbent*
in three days	in drei Tagen	*in dry tahgen*
three days ago	vor drei Tagen	*for dry tahgen*
late	spät	*shpayt*
early	früh	*froo*
soon	bald	*balt*
later on	später	*shpayter*
at the moment	im Moment	*im moment*
second	die Sekunde	*zekoonduh*
minute	die Minute	*minOOtuh*
one minute	eine Minute	*ine-uh minOOtuh*
two minutes	zwei Minuten	*tsvy minOOten*
quarter of an hour	eine Viertelstunde	*feertelshtoonduh*
half an hour	eine halbe Stunde	*halbuh shtoonduh*
three quarters of an hour	eine Dreiviertel-stunde	*dryfeertel-shtoonduh*
hour	die Stunde	*shtoonduh*
day	der Tag	*tahk*
every day	jeden Tag	*yayden tahk*
all day	den ganzen Tag	*dayn gantsen tahk*
the next day	am nächsten Tag	*am naykstenz tahk*
week	die Woche	*voKHuh*
fortnight	zwei Wochen	*tsvy voKHen*
month	der Monat	*mohnaht*
year	das Jahr	*yar*
what time is it?	wie spät ist es?	*vee shpayt ist ess*

am	morgens	*morgens*
pm	nachmittags	*nahKHmittahks*
(in the evening)	abends	*ahbents*
one o'clock	ein Uhr	*ine OOr*
ten past one	zehn nach eins	*tsayn nahKH ine-ss*
quarter past one	viertel nach eins	*feertel nahKH ine-ss*
half past one	halb zwei	*halp tsvy*
twenty to two	zwanzig vor zwei	*tsvantsish for tsvy*
quarter to two	viertel vor zwei	*feertel for tsvy*
13.00	dreizehn Uhr	*dry-tsayn OOr*
16.30	sechzehn Uhr dreißig	*zesh-tsayn OOr drysish*
at half past five	um halb sechs	*oom halp zex*

HOTELS

Hotels are categorized by the international star-rating system, with the usual range of services and level of luxury you would expect to find in the UK. If you're looking for more basic accommodation, you could try a **Gasthof**, **Gasthaus** or **Pension**. A **Gasthof** or **Gasthaus** will often have a restaurant on the ground floor and rooms on the other floors – a traditional inn. The signs '**Zimmer frei**' or '**Fremdenzimmer**' mean that rooms are available and, if on display in the window of a private house, will indicate a bed and breakfast type of accommodation.

Useful Words and Phrases

balcony	der Balkon	*balkong*
bath *(tub)*	die Badewanne	*bahduh-vannuh*
bathroom	das Bad	*baht*
bed	das Bett	*bet*
bed and breakfast	Übernachtung mit Frühstück	*ꝏbernaKHtoong mit frꝏshtꝏk*
bedroom	das (Schlaf)zimmer	*(shlahf)tsimmer*
bill	die Rechnung	*reshnoong*
breakfast	das Frühstück	*frꝏshtꝏk*
dining room	der Speisesaal	*shpyzuh-zahl*
dinner *(evening)*	das Abendessen	*ahbentessen*
double bed	das Doppelbett	*doppelbet*
double room	das Doppelzimmer	*doppeltsimmer*
foyer	das Foyer	*fwa-yay*
full board	Vollpension	*follpangz-yohn*
hotel	das Hotel	*hotel*
key	der Schlüssel	*shlꝏssel*
lift	der Aufzug, der Lift	*owf-tsook, lift*
lounge	der Aufenthaltsraum	*owfenthaltsrowm*
lunch	das Mittagessen	*mittahkessen*
maid	das Zimmermädchen	*tsimmer-maydshen*
manager	der Geschäftsführer	*gushefts-fꝏrer*
receipt	die Quittung	*kvittoong*

reception	der Empfang	*empfang*
receptionist	der Empfangschef	*empfangs-shef*
(*woman*)	die Empfangsdame	*empfangs-dahmuh*
room	das Zimmer	*tsimmer*
room service	der Zimmerservice	*tsimmer-'service'*
shower	die Dusche	*dooshuh*
single bed	das Einzelbett	*ine-tselbet*
single room	das Einzelzimmer	*ine-tsel-tsimmer*
toilet	die Toilette	*twalettuh*
twin room	das Zweibettzimmer	*tsvybet-tsimmer*
washbasin	das Waschbecken	*vashbecken*

Do you have any vacancies?
Haben Sie Zimmer frei?
hahben zee tsimmer fry

I have a reservation
Ich habe ein Zimmer reserviert
ish hahbuh ine tsimmer rezerveert

I'd like a single room
Ich möchte ein Einzelzimmer
ish murshtuh ine ine-tsel-tsimmer

I'd like a room with a bathroom/balcony
Ich möchte ein Zimmer mit Bad/Balkon
ish murshtuh ine tsimmer mit baht/balkong

Is there satellite/cable TV in the rooms?
Gibt es Satelliten/Kabel fernsehen in den Zimmern?
gipt as zateleeten/kahbel fairnzayhen in den tsimmen

I'd like a room for one night/three nights
Ich möchte ein Zimmer für eine Nacht/drei Nächte
ish murshtuh ine tsimmer fOOr ine-uh naKHt/dry neshtuh

What is the charge per night?
Was kostet es pro Nacht?
vass kostet ess pro naKHt

I don't know yet how long I'll stay
Ich weiß noch nicht, wie lange ich bleiben werde
ish vice NOKH nisht vee lang-uh ish blyben vairduh

When is breakfast/dinner?
Wann wird das Frühstück/Abendessen serviert?
vann veert dass froohshtook/ahbentessen zairveert

Please wake/call me at ... o'clock
Bitte wecken Sie mich um ... Uhr
bittuh vecken zee mish oom ... oor

Can I have breakfast in my room?
Können Sie mir das Frühstück auf mein Zimmer bringen?
kurnen zee meer dass frooshtook owf mine tsimmer bring-en

I'll be back at ... o'clock
Ich bin um ... Uhr wieder da
ish bin oom ... oor veeder da

My room number is ...
Meine Zimmernummer ist ...
mine-uh tsimmer-noommer ist

I'd like to have some laundry done
Ich möchte gern meine Wäsche waschen lassen
ish murshtuh gairn mine-uh veshuh vashen lassen

My booking was for a double room
Ich hatte ein Doppelzimmer reserviert
ish hattuh ine doppeltsimmer rezerveert

I asked for a room with an en suite bathroom
Ich hatte um ein Zimmer mit eigenem Bad gebeten
ish hattuh oom ine tsimmer mit ige-enem baht gubayten

I need a light bulb
Ich brauche eine Glühbirne
ish browKHuh ine-uh gloobeernuh

The lamp is broken
Die Lampe ist kaputt
dee lampuh ist kapoot

There is no toilet paper in the bathroom
Im Badezimmer ist kein Toilettenpapier
im bahduh-tsimmer ist kine twaletten-papeer

The window won't open
Das Fenster geht nicht auf
dass fenster gayt nisht owf

There isn't any hot water
Es gibt kein warmes Wasser
ess geept kine varmess vasser

The socket in the bathroom doesn't work
Die Steckdose im Badezimmer funktioniert nicht
dee shtek-dohzuh im bahduh-tsimmer foonkts-yoneert nisht

I'm leaving tomorrow
Ich reise morgen ab
ish ryzuh morgen ap

When do I have to vacate the room?
Bis wann muß ich das Zimmer räumen?
biss van mooss ish dass tsimmer roymen

Can I have the bill, please?
Kann ich bitte die Rechnung haben?
kan ish bittuh dee reshnoong hahben

I'll pay by credit card
Ich zahle mit Kreditkarte
ish tsahluh mit kredeetkartuh

I'll pay cash
Ich zahle in bar
ish tsahluh in bar

Can you get me a taxi?
Können Sie mir ein Taxi bestellen?
kurnen zee meer ine taxi bushtellen

Can you recommend another hotel?
Können Sie ein anderes Hotel empfehlen?
kurnen zee ine anderess hotel empfaylen

THINGS YOU'LL SEE

Aufzug	lift
Bad	bath
belegt	no vacancies
Doppelzimmer	double room
drücken	push
Dusche	shower
Eingang	entrance
Einzelzimmer	single room
Empfang	reception
Erdgeschoß	ground floor
erster Stock	first floor
Fahrstuhl	lift
Fremdenzimmer	room(s) to let
Frühstück	breakfast
Gasthaus, Gasthof	inn
Halbpension	half board
kein Zutritt	no admission
Mittagessen	lunch
Notausgang	emergency exit
nur für Gäste	patrons only
Parkplatz	car park
Pension	guesthouse
Rechnung	bill
Speisesaal	restaurant, dining room
Treppe	stairs

→

Übernachtung	night
Übernachtung mit Frühstück	bed and breakfast
voll belegt	no vacancies
Vollpension	full board
ziehen	pull
Zimmer frei	room(s) to let
Zuschlag	supplement
Zweibettzimmer	twin room
zweiter Stock	second floor

Things You'll Hear

Mit oder ohne Bad?
With or without bath?

Tut mir leid, wir sind voll belegt
I'm sorry, we're full

Es sind keine Einzelzimmer/Doppelzimmer mehr frei
There are no single/double rooms left

Für wie lange?
For how long?

Wie möchten Sie zahlen?
How would you like to pay?

Könnten Sie bitte im voraus bezahlen
Could you please pay in advance

Sie müssen das Zimmer bis zwölf Uhr räumen
You must vacate the room by midday

CAMPING AND CARAVANNING

Germany has over 2,500 well-equipped campsites, most of which are open from May until September. In some winter sports areas you will find sites open all year round.

There are also more than 600 youth hostels throughout the country, and mountain shelters or **Berghütten** (*bairk-hootten*) provided by hiking clubs, who also mark the more interesting trail routes.

Useful Words and Phrases

bucket	der Eimer	*ime-er*
campfire	das Lagerfeuer	*lahger-foy-er*
go camping	zelten gehen	*tselten gay-en*
campsite	der Campingplatz	*kemping-plats*
caravan	der Wohnwagen	*vohn-vahgen*
caravan site	der Campingplatz	*kemping-plats*
cooking utensils	die Kochgeräte	*kokh-guraytuh*
drinking water	das Trinkwasser	*trinkvasser*
groundsheet	die Zeltbodenplane	*tseltbohden-plahnuh*
hitchhike	trampen	*trempen*
rope	das Seil	*zile*
rubbish	der Abfall	*apfal*
rucksack	der Rucksack	*rookzak*
saucepans	die Kochtöpfe	*kokh-turpfuh*
sleeping bag	der Schlafsack	*shlahfzak*
tent	das Zelt	*tselt*
youth hostel	die Jugendherberge	*yoogent-hairbairguh*

Can I camp here?
Kann man hier zelten?
kan man heer tselten

Can we park the caravan here?
Können wir den Wohnwagen hier abstellen?
kurnen veer dayn vohn-vahgen heer apshtellen

Where is the nearest campsite/caravan site?
Wo ist der nächste Campingplatz/Wohnwagenplatz?
vo ist dair naykstuh kemping-plats/vohn-vahgen-plats

What is the charge per night?
Was kostet es pro Nacht?
vass kostet ess pro naKHt

How much is it for a week?
Was ist der Preis für eine Woche?
vass ist dair price fOOr ine-uh voKHuh

I only want to stay for one night
Ich möchte nur eine Nacht bleiben
ish murshtuh nOOr ine-uh naKHt blyben

We're leaving tomorrow
Wir fahren morgen ab
veer faren morgen ap

Where is the kitchen?
Wo ist die Küche?
vo ist dee kOOshuh

Can I light a fire here?
Kann man hier ein Feuer machen?
kan man heer ine foy-er maKHen

Where can I get …?
Wo bekomme ich …?
vo bukommuh ish

Is there drinking water here?
Gibt es hier Trinkwasser?
geept ess heer trinkvasser

Things You'll See

Anhänger	trailer
Ausweis	pass, identity card
Benutzung	use
Bettdecken	bedding
Campingplatz	campsite
Dusche	shower
Feuer	fire
Gebühren	charges
Jugendherberge	youth hostel
Küche	kitchen
Licht	light
Schlafraum	dormitory
Schlafsäcke	sleeping bags
Trinkwasser	drinking water
Wohnwagen	caravan
Zelt	tent
Zelten verboten	no camping
Zeltplatz	campsite
zu verleihen	for hire
zu vermieten	to rent

VILLAS AND APARTMENTS

You may be asked to pay for certain 'extras' not included in the original price. You might want to ask if electricity, gas etc is included. It's a good idea to ask about an inventory at the start, rather than be told later something is missing just as you are about to leave. You may be asked for a deposit – make sure you get a receipt for this.

Useful Words and Phrases

agent	der Vertreter	*fairtrayter*
bath	das Bad	*baht*
bathroom	das Badezimmer	*bahduhtsimmer*
bedroom	das Zimmer	*tsimmer*
blind	das Rollo	*rollo*
blocked	verstopft	*fairshtopft*
boiler	der Boiler	*'boiler'*
break *(something)*	zerbrechen	*tsairbreshen*
broken	kaputt	*kapoot*
caretaker	der Hausmeister	*howss-myster*
central heating	die Zentralheizung	*tsentrahl-hytsoong*
cleaner	die Reinemachefrau	*rynumaKHufrow*
cooker	der Herd	*hairt*
deposit	die Anzahlung	*antsahloong*
drain	der Abfluß	*apflooss*
dustbin	die Mülltonne	*mooltonnuh*
electrician	der Elektriker	*aylektriker*
electricity	der Strom	*shtrohm*
fridge	der Kühlschrank	*koolshrank*
fusebox	der Sicherungskasten	*zisheroongskasten*
gas	das Gas	*gahss*
grill	der Grill	*'grill'*
heater	das Heizgerät	*hytsgurayt*
iron	das Bügeleisen	*boogel-ize-en*

ironing board	das Bügelbrett	*bōōgelbret*
keys	die Schlüssel	*shlōōssel*
kitchen	die Küche	*kōōshuh*
leak	die undichte Stelle	*oondishtuh shtelluh*
light	das Licht	*lisht*
light bulb	die Glühbirne	*glōōbeernuh*
living room	das Wohnzimmer	*vohntsimmer*
maid	die Hausangestellte	*howss-angushtelltuh*
pillow	das Kopfkissen	*kopfkissen*
pillow slip	der Kopfkissenbezug	*kopfkissenbutsOOk*
plumber	der Klempner	*klempner*
receipt	die Quittung	*kvittoong*
refund	die Rückerstattung	*rōōkairshtattoong*
sheets	die Bettlaken	*bet-lahken*
shower	die Dusche	*dOOshuh*
sink	das Waschbecken	*vash-becken*
stopcock	der Absperrhahn	*apshpairhahn*
swimming pool	der Swimmingpool	*'swimming pool'*
tap	der Hahn	*hahn*
toilet	die Toilette	*twalettuh*
towel	das Handtuch	*hant-tOOKH*
washing machine	die Waschmaschine	*vash-masheenuh*
water	das Wasser	*vasser*
water heater	das Heißwassergerät	*hice-vasserguraytt*

Does the price include gas/electricity/cleaning?
Ist der Preis einschließlich Gas/Strom/Reinigung?
ist dair price ine-shleesslish gahss/shtrohm/rynigoong

Do I need to sign an inventory?
Muß ich eine Bestandsliste unterschreiben?
mooss ish ine-uh bushtants-listuh oontershryben

Where is this item?
Wo ist das?
vo ist dass

Please take it off the inventory
Bitte streichen Sie es von der Bestandsliste
bittuh shtryshen zee ess fon dair bushtants-listuh

We've broken this
Das ist uns kaputtgegangen
dass ist oonss kapoot-gugang-en

This was broken when we arrived
Es war schon kaputt, als wir ankamen
ess var shohn kapoot alss veer ankahmen

This was missing when we arrived
Das fehlte schon, als wir ankamen
dass fayltuh shohn alss veer ankahmen

Can I have my deposit back?
Kann ich meine Anzahlung zurückbekommen?
kan ish mine-uh antsahloong tsoorook-bukommen

Can we have an extra bed?
Können Sie uns ein extra Bett geben?
kurnen zee oonss ine extra bett gayben

Can we have more crockery/cutlery?
Können wir mehr Geschirr/Besteck bekommen?
kurnen veer mair gusheer/bushtek bukommen

Where is ...?
Wo ist ...?
vo ist

When does the maid come?
Wann kommt die Hausangestellte?
van kommt dee howss-angushtelltuh

Where can I buy/find ...?
Wo kann ich ... kaufen/finden?
vo kan ish ... kowfen/finden

When is the bank/supermarket open?
Wann hat die Bank/der Supermarkt auf?
van hat dee bank/dair zoopermarkt owf

How does the water heater work?
Wie funktioniert das Heißwassergerät?
vee foonkts-yoneert dass hice-vasserguravt

Do you do ironing/baby-sitting?
Haben Sie einen Bügeldienst/Babysitterdienst?
hahben zee ine-en boogeldeenst/'babysitter'-deenst

Do you prepare lunch/dinner?
Können Sie für uns mittags/abends kochen?
kurnen zee foor oonss mittahks/ahbents kokHen

Do we have to pay extra, or is this included in the price?
Ist das extra oder im Preis einbegriffen?
ist dass extra ohder im price ine-bugriffen

The shower doesn't work
Die Dusche funktioniert nicht
dee dooshuh foonkts-yoneert nisht

The sink is blocked
Der Abfluß ist verstopft
dair apflooss ist fairshtopft

The sink/toilet is leaking
Der Abfluß/die Toilette leckt
dair apflooss/dee twalettuh lekt

There's a burst pipe
Ein Rohr ist geplatzt
ine ror ist guplatst

The rubbish has not been collected for a week
Der Müll ist seit einer Woche nicht abgeholt worden
dair mool ist zite ine-er vokHuh nisht apguhohlt vorden

There's no electricity/gas/water
Es gibt keinen Strom/kein Gas/kein Wasser
ess geept kine-en shtrohm/kine gahss/kine vasser

Our bottled gas has run out – how do we get a new cylinder?
Unsere Gasflasche ist leer – wo bekommen wir eine neue?
oonzeruh gahss-flashuh ist lair vo bukommen veer ine-uh noyuh

Can you mend it today?
Können Sie es heute reparieren lassen?
kurnen zee ess hoytuh repareeren lassen

What is the name and telephone number of the nearest doctor/dentist?
Was ist der Name und die Telefonnummer des nächsten Arztes/Zahnarztes?
vass ist dair nahmuh oont dee telefohn-noommer des nayksten artstess/tsahn-artstess

Send your bill to …
Schicken Sie die Rechnung an …
shicken zee dee reshnoong an

I'm staying at …
Ich wohne in …
ish vohnuh in

Thanks for looking after us so well
Vielen Dank, daß Sie sich so nett um uns gekümmert haben
feelen dank dass zee zish zo nett oom oonss gukoommert hahben

See you again next year
Bis nächstes Jahr
biss naykstess yar

DRIVING

Drive on the right, overtake on the left. On dual-lane highways you may remain in the left-hand lane if there is dense traffic on your right, but when lines of traffic have formed in all lanes you are allowed to drive faster in a right-hand lane. If you happen to be in a left-hand lane you may move to the right only in order to turn off, stop or follow directional arrows.

Traffic coming from the right has priority at crossroads and junctions wherever there is no priority sign or traffic light, unless entering the main road from a car park, service station, private road, path or forest track. Your right of way is signalled by a yellow diamond or the more familiar arrow inside a red triangle. The former gives you priority for some distance ahead while the latter applies to the next intersection only. An inverted red triangle denotes that you must give way, while an octagonal STOP sign means you must stop even if there is no traffic.

In built-up areas a speed limit of 50 km/h (31 mph) is shown on a yellow plate next to the town's name. The same plate with a diagonal red stripe marks the end of both limit and area. On other roads, except dual-lane highways, there is a speed limit of 100 km/h (62 mph). Heavier vehicles – lorries, buses, cars towing caravans or trailers – are restricted to 80 km/h (50 mph) on all roads and autobahns. There is no speed limit on the autobahns for cars (with the exception of some roads in what used to be East Germany).

It is illegal to drive with only sidelights on. Motorcyclists must use dipped headlights at all times.

Some Common Road Signs

Achtung	watch out
Anlieger frei	residents only
Autobahn	motorway
Autobahndreieck	motorway junction

→

Autobahnkreuz	motorway junction
Bahnübergang	level crossing
Baustelle	roadworks
bei Frost Glatteisgefahr	icy in cold weather
bitte einordnen	get in lane
Bundesautobahn	federal motorway
Bundesstraße	A-road, trunk road
Durchgangsverkehr	through traffic
Einbahnstraße	one-way street
eingeschränktes Halteverbot	restricted parking
Fahrradweg	cycle path
Frostschäden	frost damage
Fußgänger	pedestrians
Fußgängerzone	pedestrian precinct
Gefahr	danger
gefährliche Kreuzung	dangerous junction
gefährliche Kurve	dangerous bend
Gegenverkehr hat Vorfahrt	oncoming traffic has right of way
gesperrt für Fahrzeuge aller Art	closed to all vehicles
Glatteis	black ice
Halteverbot	no stopping
Höchstgeschwindigkeit	maximum speed
keine Zufahrt	no entry
Kreuzung	crossroads
Kriechspur	crawler lane
kurvenreiche Strecke	bends
Landstraße	A-road, B-road
langsam fahren	drive slowly
Nebel	fog
nur für Busse	buses only
Parken nur mit Parkscheibe	parking disc holders only
Parkverbot	no parking

→

Radweg kreuzt	cycle track crossing
Raststätte	services area
rechts fahren	keep to the right
Sackgasse	no through road
schlechte Fahrbahn	bad surface
Schule	school
Schwerlastverkehr	heavy vehicles
Seitenstreifen nicht befahrbar	soft verges
Stadtmitte	town centre
starkes Gefälle	steep gradient
Stau	tailback, traffic jam
Steinschlag	falling rocks
Straßenbahn	tram
Überholen verboten	no overtaking
Umgehungsstraße	bypass
Umleitung	diversion
Unebenheiten	uneven surface
verengte Fahrbahn	road narrows
Vorfahrt gewähren	give way
Vorfahrtsstraße	drivers on this road have priority
Zoll	customs

Useful Words and Phrases

bonnet	die Motorhaube	*mohtorhowbuh*
boot	der Kofferraum	*kofferrowm*
brake	die Bremse	*bremzuh*
breakdown	die Panne	*pannuh*
car	das Auto	*owto*
car park	der Parkplatz	*parkplats*
(multistorey)	das Parkhaus	*parkhowss*
caravan	der Wohnwagen	*vohn-vahgen*
clutch	die Kupplung	*kooploong*
crossroads	die Kreuzung	*kroytsoong*

drive ***(verb)***	fahren	*faren*
engine	der Motor	*mohtor*
exhaust	der Auspuff	*owss-poof*
fanbelt	der Keilriemen	*kile-reemen*
garage ***(for repairs)***	die Werkstatt	*vairkshtat*
(for petrol)	die Tankstelle	*tankshtelluh*
gear	der Gang	*gang*
gears/gear box	das Getriebe	*gutreebuh*
headlights	die Scheinwerfer	*shine-vairfer*
indicator	der Blinker	*blinker*
junction	die Kreuzung	*kroytsoong*
(motorway entry)	die Auffahrt	*owf-fart*
(motorway exit)	die Ausfahrt	*owss-fart*
licence	der Führerschein	*fꝏrer-shine*
lorry	der Lastwagen	*last-vahgen*
mirror	der Spiegel	*shpeegel*
motorbike	das Motorrad	*motor-raht*
motorway	die Autobahn	*owtoh-bahn*
number plate	das Nummernschild	*noommern-shilt*
parking meter	die Parkuhr	*park-oor*
parking ticket	der Strafzettel	*shtrahf-tsettel*
petrol	das Benzin	*bentseen*
petrol station	die Tankstelle	*tankshtelluh*
rear lights	das Rücklicht	*rꝏklisht*
road	die Straße	*shtrahssuh*
spares	die Ersatzteile	*airzats-tile-uh*
spark plug	die Zündkerze	*tsꝏnt-kairtsuh*
speed	die Geschwindigkeit	*gushvindish-kite*
speedometer	der Tacho(meter)	*takho(mayter)*
steering wheel	das Lenkrad	*lenkraht*
tow	abschleppen	*apshleppen*
traffic lights	die Ampel	*ampel*
trailer	der Anhänger	*anheng-er*
tyre	der Reifen	*rife-en*
van	der Lieferwagen	*leefer-vahgen*
wheel	das Rad	*raht*

windscreen	die Windschutz-scheibe	*vint-shoots-shybuh*
windscreen wiper	der Scheibenwischer	*shyben-visher*

I'd like some petrol/oil/water
Ich brauche Benzin/Öl/Wasser
ish browKHuh bentseen/url/vasser

Fill it up, please!
Volltanken bitte!
folltanken bittuh

20 litres of 4-star unleaded, please
Zwanzig Liter Super bleifrei bitte
tsvantsish leeter zooper bly-fry bittuh

Would you check the tyres, please?
Könnten Sie bitte die Reifen überprüfen?
kurnten zee bittuh dee rife-en ooberproofen

Do you do repairs?
Machen Sie Reparaturen?
maKHen zee reparatooren

Can you repair the clutch?
Können Sie die Kupplung reparieren?
kurnen zee dee kooploong repareeren

There is something wrong with the engine
Mit dem Motor stimmt etwas nicht
mit daym mohtor shtimmt etvass nisht

The engine is overheating
Der Motor ist heißgelaufen
dair mohtor ist hice-gulowfen

I need a new tyre
Ich brauche einen neuen Reifen
ish browKHuh ine-en noyen rife-en

Can you replace this?
Haben Sie dafür einen Ersatz?
hahben zee dafoor ine-en airsats

The indicator is not working
Der Blinker funktioniert nicht
dair blinker foonkts-yoneert nisht

How long will it take?
Wie lange wird das dauern?
vee lang-uh veert dass dowern

Where can I park?
Wo kann ich parken?
vo kan ish parken

Can I park here?
Kann ich hier parken?
kan ish heer parken

I'd like to hire a car
Ich möchte ein Auto mieten
ish murshtuh ine owto meeten

I'd like an automatic/a manual
Ich möchte ein Auto mit Automatik/mit Handschaltung
ish murshtuh ine owto mit owtomahtik/mit hantshaltoong

Can we hire a baby/child seat?
Können wir einen Baby/Kindersitz mieten?
kurnnen veer ine-nen baibee/kindairzits meeten

For one day/two days/one week
Für einen Tag/zwei Tage/eine Woche
foor ine-en tahk/tsvy tahguh/ine-uh voKHuh

How much is it for one day?
Was kostet es pro Tag?
vass kostet ess pro tahk

Is there a mileage charge?
Wird ein Preis pro Kilometer erhoben?
veert ine price pro kilomayter airhohben

When do I have to return it?
Wann muß ich es wieder zurückbringen?
van mooss ish ess veeder tsoorookbring-en

Where is the nearest petrol station?
Wo ist die nächste Tankstelle?
vo ist dee naykstuh tankshtelluh

How do I get to ...?
Wie komme ich nach ...?
vee kommuh ish nahKH

Is this the road to ...?
Ist das die Straße nach ...?
ist dass dee shtrahssuh nahKH

Which is the quickest way to ...?
Was ist der schnellste Weg zum ...?
vass ist dair shnelstuh vayk tsoom

Directions You May Be Given

an der nächsten Ausfahrt	at the next junction
an der nächsten Kreuzung	at the next crossroads
erste Straße rechts	first on the right
geradeaus	straight on
links	on the left
links abbiegen	turn left
rechts	on the right
rechts abbiegen	turn right
vorbei an ...	past the ...
zweite Straße links	second on the left

THINGS YOU'LL SEE

Ausfahrt	exit
Autowäsche	car wash
Benzin	petrol
bleifrei	lead free
Bremsflüssigkeit	brake fluid
Einfahrt	entrance, way in
Geschwindigkeits-beschränkung	speed limit
LKW	heavy goods vehicle, HGV
Luftdruck	air pressure
Motor abstellen	switch off engine
Münztank	coin-operated pump
Öl	oil
Parkhaus	multistorey car park
Parkplatz	car park
Parkschein entnehmen	take a ticket
PKW	private car
Reifendruck	tyre pressure
Reparaturwerkstatt	garage, repairs
Schritt fahren	drive at walking speed
Super	4-star
Tankstelle	petrol station
unverbleit	unleaded
verbleit	leaded
Waschstraße	car wash
Wasser	water
Zapfsäule	petrol pump

YOU MAY HEAR

Kann ich bitte Ihren Führerschein sehen?
May I see your driving licence, please?

TRAVELLING AROUND

Air Travel

In addition to an excellent domestic network, air services connect the following German cities with many UK and USA destinations: Berlin, Bremen, Cologne (**Köln**), Bonn, Düsseldorf, Frankfurt am Main, Hamburg, Hanover, Leipzig, Munich (**München**), Nuremberg (**Nürnberg**) and Stuttgart.

Rail Travel

The German Federal Railways or **DB** (**Deutsche Bundesbahn**) are outstanding for their punctuality and general efficiency. International trains connect Germany with most parts of Europe, while fast, regular Inter-City and express trains link the larger German towns and cities. The main types of train are:

TEE	Trans European Express
IC	Inter-City
D	Express
E(**Eilzug**)	Semi-fast train
Personenzug	Local train – stopping at every station

A supplement, or **Zuschlag** (*tsooshlahk*), is payable for all journeys by **TEE** and **IC** trains, and on some **D** trains for journeys under 50km.

Local Transport, Boat Travel

There are good bus and tram networks in all German towns and cities. Single tickets can be bought from a ticket machine located by the bus or tram stop, or sometimes from the driver. It is usually cheaper to buy a multi-journey ticket from a ticket machine. If you need to change buses or trams en route it is not necessary to buy another ticket. In some cities you will also have to stamp your ticket in a ticket-stamping machine situated on board the bus or tram – you will have to do this if you have bought a multi-journey ticket.

Some of the larger cities such as Hamburg, Munich, Berlin, Frankfurt, Cologne and Nuremberg have an underground system or **U-Bahn** (*oobahn*), and some cities also have a fast local rail network or **S-Bahn** (*ess-bahn*). Zone systems also operate in major cities, a flat fare applying in each zone with the fare increasing according to the number of zones crossed. Tickets can be obtained from automatic ticket machines, most of which give change.

A number of rural bus services are also run by the German Federal Railways and Federal Post. Post buses are yellow, while those belonging to the Federal Railways are red.

A more leisurely way of travelling in Germany, especially during the summer months, is on one of the steamer services operating on the major rivers such as the Rhine (**der Rhein**), Moselle (**die Mosel**, *mohzel*) and Danube (**die Donau**, *dohnow*) and on Lake Constance (**der Bodensee**, *bohdenzay*), the Bavarian lakes and the Berlin lakes.

Taxis

Taxis are normally hired from a taxi rank or by telephone. It is not customary in Germany to hail a taxi on the street.

Useful Words and Phrases

airport	der Flughafen	*flook-hahfen*
airport bus	der Flughafenbus	*flook-hahfenbooss*
aisle seat	der Sitz am Gang	*sits am gang*
adult	der Erwachsene	*airvaksenuh*
baggage claim	die Gepäckausgabe	*gupek-owssgahbuh*
boarding card	die Bordkarte	*bort-kartuh*
boat	das Schiff	*shiff*
booking office	der Fahrkarten-schalter	*farkarten-shalter*
bus	der Bus	*booss*
bus station	der Busbahnhof	*boossbahnhohf*
bus stop	die Bushaltestelle	*booss-haltuh-shtelluh*

carriage	der Wagen	*vahgen*
check-in desk	der Abfertigungs-schalter	*apfairtigoongs-shalter*
child	das Kind	*kint*
coach *(bus)*	der Bus	*booss*
compartment	das Abteil	*aptile*
connection	die Verbindung	*fairbindoong*
cruise	die Kreuzfahrt	*kroyts-fart*
Customs	der Zoll	*tsoll*
departure lounge	die Abflughalle	*apfLOOk-halluh*
domestic	Inland-	*inlant-*
emergency exit	der Notausgang	*noht-owssgang*
(on plane)	der Notausstieg	*noht-owss-shteek*
entrance	der Eingang	*ine-gang*
exit	der Ausgang	*owssgang*
fare	der Fahrpreis	*farprice*
ferry	die Fähre	*fayruh*
first class	die erste Klasse	*airstuh klassuh*
flight	der Flug	*flook*
flight number	die Flugnummer	*flooknoommer*
gate	der Flugsteig	*flook-shtike*
hand luggage	das Handgepäck	*hant-gupek*
international	international	*internats-yonahl*
left luggage office	die Gepäck-aufbewahrung	*gupek-owfbuva roong*
lost property office	das Fundbüro	*foont-bœro*
luggage trolley	der Gepäckkarren	*gupek-karren*
network map	der Netzplan	*netsplahn*
non-smoking	Nichtraucher	*nishtrowKHer*
number 5 bus	der Bus Nr. 5	*booss noommer fœnf*
passport	der Paß	*pas*
platform	der Bahnsteig	*bahn-shtike*
railway	die Eisenbahn	*ize-en-bahn*

reserved seat	der reservierte Platz	*rezerveertuh plats*
restaurant car	der Speisewagen	*shpyzuh-vahgen*
return ticket	die Rückfahrkarte	*rookfarkartuh*
seat	der Platz	*plats*
second class	die zweite Klasse	*tsvytuh klassuh*
single ticket	die einfache Fahrkarte	*ine-faKHuh farkartuh*
sleeper car	der Schlafwagen	*shlahf-vahgen*
smoking	Raucher	*rowKHer*
station	der Bahnhof	*bahnhohf*
taxi	das Taxi	*taxi*
terminus	die Endstation	*ent-shtats-yohn*
ticket	die Fahrkarte	*farkartuh*
(air)	das Ticket	*'ticket'*
timetable	der Fahrplan	*farplahn*
train	der Zug	*tsook*
tram	die Straßenbahn	*shtrahssenbahn*
underground	die U-Bahn	*oobahn*
waiting room	der Wartesaal	*vartuh-zahl*
window seat	der Fensterplatz	*fensterplats*

AIR TRAVEL

I'd like a non-smoking seat, please
Ich möchte gern einen Nichtraucherplatz
ish murshtuh gairn ine-en nisht-rowKHerplats

I'd like a window seat, please
Ich möchte gern einen Fensterplatz
ish murshtuh gairn ine-en fensterplats

How long will the flight be delayed?
Wie lange dauert die Verspätung?
vee lang-uh veert dowert dee fairshpehtoong

Which gate for the flight to …?
Von welchem Flugsteig fliegt die Maschine nach …?
fon velshem flook-shtike fleekt dee masheenuh nahKH

RAIL, BUS AND UNDERGROUND TRAVEL

When does the train/bus for Frankfurt leave?
Wann fährt der Zug/Bus nach Frankfurt ab?
van fairt dair tsOOk/booss nahKH frankfoort ap

When does the train/bus from Munich arrive?
Wann kommt der Zug/Bus aus München an?
van kommt dair tsOOk/booss owss mOOnshen an

When is the next train/bus to Nuremberg?
Wann fährt der nächste Zug/Bus nach Nürnberg?
van fairt dair naykstuh tsOOk/booss nahKH nOOrnbairk

When is the first train/bus to Pforzheim?
Wann fährt der erste Zug/Bus nach Pforzheim?
van fairt dair airstuh tsOOk/booss nahKH pforts-hime

When is the last train/bus to Cologne?
Wann fährt der letzte Zug/Bus nach Köln?
van fayrt dair letstuh tsOOk/booss nahKH kurln

What is the fare to Heidelberg?
Was kostet die Fahrt nach Heidelberg?
vass kostet dee fart nahKH hydelbairk

Do I have to change?
Muß ich umsteigen?
mooss ish oomshtygen

Does the train/bus stop at Lüneburg?
Hält der Zug/Bus in Lüneburg?
helt dair tsOOk/booss in lOOnuh-boork

How long does it take to get to Dresden?
Wie lange dauert die Fahrt nach Dresden?
vee lang-uh dowert dee fart nahKH draysden

Where can I buy a ticket?
Wo kann ich eine Fahrkarte lösen?
vo kan ish ine-uh farkartuh lurzen

A single/return ticket to Bremen, please
Eine einfache Fahrkarte/eine Rückfahrkarte nach Bremen, bitte
ine-uh ine-faKHuh farkartuh/ine-uh rœckfarkartuh nahKH braymen bittuh

Could you help me get a ticket?
Könnten Sie mir bitte helfen, eine Fahrkarte zu lösen?
kurnten zee meer bittuh helfen ine-uh farkartuh tsoo lurzen

Do I have to pay a supplement?
Muß ich einen Zuschlag zahlen?
mooss ish ine-en tsooshlahk tsahlen

Do we have to pay for the children?
Müssen Kinder auch Eintritt bezahlen?
murssen kindair owKH ine-tritt betsahlen

Is there a family ticket available?
Gibt es eine Familienkarte?
gipt as ine-nuh fahmeelee-ankahrte

I'd like to reserve a seat
Ich möchte gern einen Platz reservieren
ish murshtuh gairn ine-en plats rezerveeren

Is this the right train/bus for Bonn?
Ist das der Zug/Bus nach Bonn?
ist dass dair tsook/booss nahKH bon

Is this the right platform for the Wiesbaden train?
Ist das das Gleis für den Zug nach Wiesbaden?
ist dass dass glice fœr dayn tsook nahKH veessbahden

Which platform for the Düsseldorf train?
Von welchem Gleis fährt der Zug nach Düsseldorf?
fon velshem glice fairt dair tsook nahKH dœsseldorf

Is the train/bus late?
Hat der Zug/Bus Verspätung?
hat dair tsook/booss fairshpaytoong

Could you help me with my luggage, please?
Könnten Sie mir bitte mit meinem Gepäck helfen?
kurnten zee meer bittuh mit mine-em gupek helfen

Is this a non-smoking compartment?
Ist das ein Nichtraucherabteil?
ist dass ine nishtrowKHer-aptile

Is this seat free?
Ist dieser Platz frei?
ist deezer plats fry

This seat is taken
Dieser Platz ist besetzt
deezer plats ist buzetst

I have reserved this seat
Ich habe eine Reservierung für diesen Platz
ish hahbuh ine-uh rezerveeroong foor deezen plats

May I open/close the window?
Kann ich das Fenster öffnen/schließen?
kan ish dass fenster urfnen/shleessen

When do we arrive in Saarbrücken?
Wann kommen wir in Saarbrücken an?
van kommen veer in zarbrooken an

What station is this?
Wo sind wir hier?
vo zint veer heer

Do we stop at Singen?
Halten wir in Singen?
halten veer in zing-en

Is there a restaurant car on this train?
Hat dieser Zug einen Speisewagen?
hat deezer tsook ine-en shpyzuh-vahgen

Replies You May Be Given

Der nächste Zug fährt um neun Uhr dreißig
The next train leaves at nine thirty

Umsteigen in Darmstadt
Change at Darmstadt

Sie müssen einen Zuschlag zahlen
You have to pay a supplement

Es sind keine Plätze mehr frei
There are no more seats available

Where is the nearest underground station?
Wo ist die nächste U-Bahn-Station?
vo ist dee naykstuh oobahn-shtats-yohn

Where is the bus station?
Wo ist der Busbahnhof?
vo ist dair boossbahnhohf

Which buses go to Baden-Baden?
Welche Busse fahren nach Baden-Baden?
velshuh boossuh faren nahKH bahden-bahden

How often do the buses to Travemünde run?
Wie oft fahren die Busse nach Travemünde?
vee oft faren dee boossuh nahKH trahvuh-moonduh

Will you let me know when we're there?
Sagen Sie mir bitte Bescheid, wenn wir da sind?
zahgen zee meer bittuh bushite ven veer da zint

Do I have to get off here?
Muß ich hier aussteigen?
mooss ish heer owss-shtygen

How do you get to Bad Homburg?
Wie komme ich am besten nach Bad Homburg?
vee kommuh ish am besten nahKH baht homboork

I want to go to Hamelin
Ich möchte nach Hameln fahren
ish murshtuh nahKH hahmeln faren

Do you go near Wildbad?
Fahren Sie in die Nähe von Wildbad?
faren zee in dee nay-uh fon viltbaht

TAXIS

To the airport, please
Zum Flughafen bitte
tsoom flookhahfen bittuh

How much will it cost?
Wieviel kostet das?
vee-feel kostet dass

Could you stop just here?
Können Sie hier halten, bitte
kurnen zee heer halten bittuh

Could you wait for a moment then take me back?
Können Sie hier einen Moment warten, und mich dann wieder zurückfahren?
kurnen zee heer ine-en moment varten oont mish dan veeder tsoorookfaren

THINGS YOU'LL SEE

Abfahrt	departure(s)
Abfertigung	check-in
Abflug	departure(s)
Ankunft	arrival(s)
Ausgang	departure, exit
Auskunft	information
Ausland	international
außer sonntags	Sundays excepted
Ausweis	pass
Bahnhofsmission	office providing help for travellers in difficulty
Bahnhofspolizei	railway police
Bahnsteig	platform
Bahnsteigkarte	platform ticket
Behinderte	disabled persons
besetzt	engaged
bezahlen	to pay
bitte anschnallen	fasten seat belt
Damen	women
DB (Deutsche Bundesbahn)	German railways
Direktflug	direct flight
einchecken	to check in
einfache Fahrt	single journey
Einstieg nur mit Fahrausweis	obtain a ticket before boarding
Einstieg vorn/hinten	entrance at front/rear
einwerfen	to insert
Endstation	terminus
Entwerter	ticket stamping machine
Erwachsene	adults
Fahrausweis	ticket
Fahrer	driver
Fahrgäste	passengers

→

Fahrkarte	ticket
Fahrkartenautomat	ticket machine
Fahrkartenschalter	tickets, ticket office
Fahrplan	timetable
Fahrschein	ticket
Fahrscheinkauf vom Fahrer	buy your ticket from the driver
Fahrt	journey
Flug	flight
Flugdauer	flight time
Flughafenbus	airport bus
Flugplan	timetable
Flugsteig	gate
frei	vacant
Geldeinwurf	insert money here
Geldrückgabe	returned coins
Gepäckaufbewahrung	left luggage
Gepäckausgabe	baggage claim
Gepäckschließfächer	luggage lockers
gesperrt	closed, no entry
Gleis	platform
Hafen	harbour
Hafenrundfahrt	boat trip round the harbour
hält nicht in …	does not stop in …
Haltestelle	stop
Hauptbahnhof (Hbf)	central station
Herren	men
hier einsteigen	enter here
Imbiß	snacks
Inland	domestic
kein Ausstieg	no exit
kein Einstieg	exit only, enter by other door
kein Zugang	no entry
Kinder	children
Kurzstrecke	short distance (with a lower fare)

→

Linie	line, airline
Linienflug	scheduled flight
Mehrfahrtenkarte	multi-journey ticket
Mißbrauch strafbar	penalty for misuse
Monatskarte	monthly ticket
Münzen	coins
Nah(Schnell)verkehrszug	local train
Netzkarte	travelcard
nicht hinauslehnen	do not lean out of the window
nicht rauchen	no smoking
Nichtraucher	non-smokers
Notausgang	emergency exit
Notausstieg	emergency exit
Notbremse	emergency brake
nur werktags	weekdays only
Ortszeit	local time
Passagiere	passengers
passendes Fahrgeld	exact fare
Paßkontrolle	passport control
Platzkarte	seat reservation
Rauchen verboten	no smoking
Raucher	smokers
Reiseauskunft	travel information
reserviert	reserved
Sammelkarte	multi-journey ticket
samstags	on Saturdays
S-Bahn	local railway system
Schlafwagen	sleeper
Schließfächer	luggage lockers
Sitzplätze	seats
sonn- und feiertags	on Sundays and public holidays
Speisewagen	restaurant car
Stehplätze	standing room
Strecke	route

→

Tageskarte	day ticket
U-Bahn	underground
U-Bahnhof	underground station
umsteigen	to change
Verspätung	delay
Wagen	carriage
Wagenstandanzeiger	order of cars
Wartesaal	waiting room
Wechselstube	currency exchange
zahlen	to pay
Zeitungen/Zeitschriften	newspapers/magazines
Zoll	customs
zu den Zügen	to the trains
zuschlagpflichtig	supplement must be paid
Zwischenlandung	intermediate stop

THINGS YOU'LL HEAR

Haben Sie Gepäck?
Do you have any luggage?

Raucher oder Nichtraucher?
Smoking or non-smoking?

Fenstersitz oder Sitz am Gang?
Window seat or aisle seat?

Kann ich bitte Ihren Paß/Ihr Ticket sehen?
Can I see your passport/ticket, please?

Die Passagiere werden gebeten, sich zum Flugsteig 7 zu begeben
Passengers are requested to proceed to gate 7

Erster/letzter Aufruf für Flug BA302 nach Birmingham
First/last call for flight BA302 to Birmingham

→

Achtung!
Attention!

Bitte einsteigen
Board the train

Der Zug nach Lübeck hat Einfahrt nach Gleis 7
The train for Lübeck is approaching platform 7

Vorsicht bei der Einfahrt des Zuges
Please stand well clear of the approaching train

Planmäßige Ankunft: 13 Uhr 50
Scheduled arrival: 13.50

Der Zug hält nicht in Brühl
The train does not stop in Brühl

Der Zug fährt sofort ab
The train is now leaving

Der Zug hat zehn Minuten Verspätung
The train is ten minutes late

Bitte von der Bahnsteigkante zurücktreten
Please stand clear of the edge of the platform

Einsteigen und Türen schließen
Board the train and close the doors

Die Fahrkarten bitte
Tickets, please

Noch jemand zugestiegen?
Any more tickets?

EATING OUT

In Germany you'll find a wide range of places to eat, from the gourmet restaurant to the sausage and chips kiosk on the pavement. Fast food outlets, Chinese, Italian and Greek restaurants will be familiar. Not so perhaps the **Balkangrill**, serving spicy dishes from the Balkan countries.

If you want something typically German you could do a lot worse than try a small **Gasthaus** (*gast-howss*), or inn. Some dishes vary from region to region, but one shared characteristic you'll find is that German portions are not skimpy. Germans tend to eat a lot of meat; vegetarians might have to make a special request.

Ask for a small beer (**ein kleines Bier**, *ine kline-ess beer*) and you'll normally get a glass of around 0.2 litres. A large beer (**ein großes Bier**, *ine grohss-ess beer*) will normally be 0.4 or 0.5 litres, although in Bavaria you may well get a litre, which is known as **eine Maß** (*ine-uh mahss*). German beer is usually **Pils**. In some areas you might try **Alt**, which is a darker beer. German wine is either **süß** (*sooss*, 'sweet'), **trocken** (*trocken*, 'dry') or, if you like it dry and a little sharper, **herb** (*hairp*). If you'd like to try a local wine, ask for **einen Wein aus dieser Gegend** (*ine-en vine owss deezer gaygent*).

If you're having a drink in a pub or bar you don't pay when ordering. Instead, the barman or barmaid will keep a tally of what you've bought, often ticking it off on your beer mat. If you sit at a table, you can expect table service (for no extra charge). There are no restrictions on taking children into pubs.

Useful Words and Phrases

beer	das Bier	*beer*
bill	die Rechnung	*reshnoong*
bottle	die Flasche	*flashuh*
bread	das Brot	*broht*
butter	die Butter	*bootter*

café	das Café	*kaffay*
cake	der Kuchen	*kOOKHen*
carafe	die Karaffe	*karaffuh*
children's portion	der Kinderteller	*kinderteller*
coffee	der Kaffee	*kaffay*
cup	die Tasse	*tassuh*
dessert	das Dessert	*dessair*
fork	die Gabel	*gahbel*
glass	das Glas	*glahss*
half-litre	der halbe Liter	*halbuh leeter*
knife	das Messer	*messer*
main course	das Hauptgericht	*howpt-gurisht*
menu	die Speisekarte	*shpyzuh-kartuh*
milk	die Milch	*milsh*
pepper	der Pfeffer	*pfeffer*
plate	der Teller	*teller*
receipt	die Quittung	*kvittoong*
restaurant	das Restaurant	*restorong*
salt	das Salz	*zalts*
sandwich	das belegte Brot	*bulayktuh broht*
serviette	die Serviette	*zairvee-ettuh*
snack	der Imbiß	*imbiss*
soup	die Suppe	*zooppuh*
spoon	der Löffel	*lurfel*
starter	die Vorspeise	*forshpyzuh*
sugar	der Zucker	*tsooker*
table	der Tisch	*tish*
tea	der Tee	*tay*
teaspoon	der Teelöffel	*taylurfel*
tip	das Trinkgeld	*trinkgelt*
waiter	der Ober	*ohber*
waitress	die Bedienung	*budeenoong*
water	das Wasser	*vasser*
wine	der Wein	*vine*
wine list	die Weinkarte	*vine-kartuh*

A table for one/two/three, please
Einen Tisch für eine Person/zwei/drei Personen, bitte
ine-en tish foor ine-uh pairzohn/tsvy/dry pairzohnen bittuh

Can I see the menu/wine list?
Könnte ich bitte die Speisekarte/Weinkarte haben?
kurntuh ish bittuh dee shpyzuh-kartuh/vine-kartuh hahben

What would you recommend?
Was könnten Sie empfehlen?
vass kurnten zee empfaylen

I'd like ...
Ich hätte gern ...
ish hettuh gairn

Just a cup of coffee, please
Nur eine Tasse Kaffee, bitte
noor ine-uh tassuh kaffay bittuh

I only want a snack
Ich möchte nur eine Kleinigkeit
ish murshtuh noor ine-uh kline-ishkite

Is there a set menu?
Gibt es ein Tagesgericht?
geept ess ine tahges-gurisht

A litre carafe of house red, please
Einen Liter roten Tafelwein, bitte
ine-en leeter rohten tahfel-vine bittuh

Do you have any vegetarian dishes?
Haben Sie vegetarische Gerichte?
hahben zee vegetarishuh gurishtuh

Could we have some water, please?
Könnten Sie uns ein Glas Wasser geben?
kurnten zee oonss ine glas vasser gayben

Two more beers, please
Noch zwei Bier, bitte
nokh tsvy beer bittuh

Do you do children's portions?
Gibt es auch Kinderteller?
geept ess owkh kinderteller

Is there a highchair/baby changing room?
Gibt es dort einen Hochstuhl/einen Wickelraum?
gipt as dohrt ine-nen hokhshtuhl/ine-nen vikkelrowm

Can you warm this bottle/baby food for me?
Können Sie diese Flasche/Babynahrung für mich aufwärmen?
kurnnen zee deezuh flahshuh/baibee-nahrunk foor mish owf-vayrmen

Waiter/Waitress!
Herr Ober!/Fräulein!
hair ohber/froyline

We didn't order this
Das haben wir nicht bestellt
dass hahben veer nisht bushtellt

I'm still waiting for my dessert
Ich warte noch auf mein Dessert
ish vahrtuh nokh owf mine dessair

May we have some more ...?
Könnten wir noch etwas ... haben?
kurnten veer nokh etvass ... hahben

Can I have a different knife/fork?
Kann ich bitte ein anderes Messer/eine andere Gabel haben?
kan ish bittuh ine anderess messer/ine-uh anderuh gahbel hahben

Can we have the bill, please?
Zahlen, bitte
tsahlen bittuh

Could I have a receipt, please?
Könnte ich bitte eine Quittung bekommen?
kurntuh ish bittuh ine-uh kvittoong bukommen

Can we pay separately?
Können wir getrennt bezahlen?
kurnen veer gutrennt butsahlen

The meal was very good, thank you
Es hat sehr gut geschmeckt, vielen Dank
es hat zair goot gushmeckt feelen dank

THINGS YOU'LL HEAR

Guten Appetit!
Enjoy your meal!

Was möchten Sie trinken?
What would you like to drink?

Hat es Ihnen geschmeckt?
Did you enjoy your meal?

THINGS YOU'LL SEE

Bedienung inbegriffen	service included
Bierkeller	beer cellar
Eiscafé	ice cream parlour (also serves coffee and liqueurs)
Gaststätte	inn, small restaurant, pub
Ratskeller	restaurant and bar close to town hall
Schnellimbiß	take-away, snack bar (no seating)
Tageskarte	menu of the day
Weinstube	wine bar (traditional style)
Wirtshaus	pub

MENU GUIDE

Aal	eel
Aalsuppe	eel soup
am Spieß	on the spit
Ananas	pineapple
Äpfel	apples
Apfel im Schlafrock	baked apple in puff pastry
Apfelkompott	stewed apples
Apfelmus	apple purée
Apfelsaft	apple juice
Apfelsinen	oranges
Apfelstrudel	apple strudel
Apfeltasche	apple turnover
Apfelwein	cider
Aprikosen	apricots
Arme Ritter	bread soaked in milk and egg then fried
Artischocken	artichokes
Aspik	aspic
Auberginen	aubergines
Auflauf	(baked) pudding or omelette
Aufschnitt	sliced cold meats, cold cuts
Austern	oysters
Backobst	dried fruit
Backpflaume	prune
Baiser	meringue
Balkansalat	cabbage and pepper salad
Bananen	bananas
Bandnudeln	ribbon noodles
Basilikum	basil
Bauernauflauf	bacon and potato omelette
Bauernfrühstück	bacon and potato omelette
Bauernomelett	bacon and potato omelette
Bechamelkartoffeln	sliced potatoes in creamy sauce
Bechamelsoße	creamy sauce with onions and ham
Bedienung	service
Beilagen	side dishes
Berliner	jam doughnut
Bier	beer
Birnen	pears

Biskuit	sponge cake
Biskuitrolle	Swiss roll
Bismarckhering	filleted pickled herring
Blätterteig	puff pastry
blau	boiled
Blaukraut	red cabbage
Blumenkohl	cauliflower
Blumenkohlsuppe	cauliflower soup
blutig	rare
Blutwurst	black pudding
Bockwurst	large frankfurter
Bohnen	beans
Bohneneintopf	bean stew
Bohnensalat	bean salad
Bohnensuppe	bean soup
Bouillon	clear soup
Bouletten	meatballs
Braten	roast meat
Bratensoße	gravy
Brathering	(pickled) fried herring (served cold)
Bratkartoffeln	fried potatoes
Bratwurst	grilled pork sausage
Brot	bread
Brötchen	roll
Brühwurst	large frankfurter
Brust	breast
Bückling	smoked red herring
Bunte Platte	mixed platter
Burgundersoße	Burgundy wine sauce
Buttercremetorte	cream cake
Buttermilch	buttermilk
Champignons	mushrooms
Champignonsoße	mushroom sauce
Chinakohl	Chinese cabbage
Cordon bleu	veal cordon bleu
Currywurst mit Pommes frites	curried pork sausage with chips
Dampfnudeln	sweet yeast dumpling
Deutsches Beefsteak	mince patty, minced meat
Dicke Bohnen	broad beans
Dillsoße	dill sauce
durchgebraten	well-done

durchwachsen	with fat
durchwachsener Speck	streaky bacon
Eier	eggs
Eierauflauf	omelette
Eierkuchen	pancake
Eierpfannkuchen	pancake
Eierspeise	egg dish
eingelegt	pickled
Eintopf	stew
Eintopfgericht	stew
Eis	ice
Eisbecher	sundae
Eisbein	knuckles of pork
Eisschokolade	iced chocolate
Eissplittertorte	ice chip cake
Endiviensalat	endive salad
englisch	rare
Entenbraten	roast duck
entgrätet	boned
Erbsen	peas
Erbsensuppe	pea soup
Erdbeertorte	strawberry cake
Essig	vinegar
Falscher Hase	meat loaf
Fasan	pheasant
Feldsalat	lamb's lettuce
Fenchel	fennel
Fett	fat
Filet	fillet (steak)
Fisch	fish
Fischfilet	fish fillet
Fischfrikadellen	fishcakes
Fischstäbchen	fish fingers
Flädlesuppe	consommé with pancake strips
flambiert	flambéed
Fleischbrühe	bouillon
Fleischkäse	meat loaf
Fleischklößchen	meatball(s)
Fleischpastete	meat vol-au-vent
Fleischsalat	diced meat salad with mayonnaise
Fleischwurst	pork sausage

Fond	meat juices
Forelle	trout
Forelle blau	boiled trout
Forelle Müllerin (Art)	trout with butter and lemon (breaded)
Frikadelle	rissole
Frikassee	fricassee
fritiert	(deep-) fried
Froschschenkel	frog's legs
Fruchtsaft	fruit juice
Frühlingsrolle	spring roll
Gans	goose
Gänsebraten	roast goose
Gänseleber	goose liver
Gänseleberpastete	goose-liver pâté
garniert	garnished
Gebäck	pastries, cakes
gebacken	baked
gebraten	roast
gebunden	thickened
gedünstet	steamed
Geflügel	poultry
Geflügelleber	chicken liver
Geflügelleberragout	chicken liver ragoût
gefüllt	stuffed
gefüllte Kalbsbrust	veal roll
gekocht	boiled
gekochter Schinken	boiled ham
Gelee	jelly
gemischter Salat	mixed salad
Gemüse	vegetable(s)
Gemüseplatte	assorted vegetables
Gemüsereis	rice with vegetables
Gemüsesalat	vegetable salad
Gemüsesuppe	vegetable soup
gepökelt	salted, pickled
geräuchert	smoked
Gericht	dish
geschmort	braised; stewed
Geschnetzeltes	strips of meat in thick sauce
Geselchtes	salted and smoked meat
gespickt	larded

Getränke	beverages
Gewürze	spices
Gewürzgurken	gherkins
Goldbarsch	type of perch
Götterspeise	jelly
gratiniert	au gratin
Grieß	semolina
Grießklößchen	semolina dumplings
Grießpudding	semolina pudding
Grießsuppe	semolina soup
grüne Bohnen	French beans
grüne Nudeln	green pasta
grüner Aal	fresh eel
Grünkohl	(curly) kale
Gulasch	goulash
Gulaschsuppe	goulash soup
Gurkensalat	cucumber salad
Hackfleisch	mince
Hähnchen	chicken
Hähnchenkeule	chicken leg
Haifischflossensuppe	shark-fin soup
Hammelbraten	roast mutton
Hammelfleisch	mutton
Hammelkeule	leg of mutton
Hammelrücken	saddle of mutton
Hartkäse	hard cheese
Haschee	hash
Hasenkeule	haunch of hare
Hasenpfeffer	hare casserole
Hauptspeisen	main courses
Hausfrauenart	home-made style
Hausmacher (Art)	home-made style
Hecht	pike
Heidelbeeren	bilberries, blueberries
Heilbutt	halibut
Heringssalat	herring salad
Heringsstipp	herring salad
Heringstopf	pickled herrings in sauce
Herz	heart
Herzragout	heart ragoût
Himbeeren	raspberries

Himmel und Erde	potato and apple purée with black pudding or liver sausage
Hirn	brains
Hirschbraten	roast venison
Hirschmedaillons	small venison fillets
Honig	honey
Honigkuchen	honey cake
Honigmelone	honeydew melon
Hoppelpoppel	bacon and potato omelette
Hüfte	haunch
Huhn	chicken
Hühnerbrühe	chicken broth
Hühnerfrikassee	chicken fricassee
Hühnersuppe	chicken soup
Hülsenfrüchte	peas and beans, pulses
Hummer	lobster
Jägerschnitzel	cutlet with mushrooms
Kabeljau	cod
Kaffee	coffee
Kaiserschmarren	sugared pancake with raisins
Kakao	cocoa
Kalbfleisch	veal
Kalbsbraten	roast veal
Kalbsbries	sweetbread
Kalbsfrikassee	veal fricassee
Kalbshaxe	leg of veal
Kalbsmedaillons	small veal fillets
Kalbsnierenbraten	roast veal with kidney
Kalbsschnitzel	veal cutlet
kalte Platte	cold meal
kalter Braten	cold roast meat
kaltes Büfett	cold buffet
Kaltschale	cold sweet soup made from fruit
Kaninchen	rabbit
Kaninchenbraten	roast rabbit
Kapern	capers
Karamelpudding	caramel pudding
Karotten	carrots
Karpfen	carp
Kartoffelbrei	potato purée
Kartoffelklöße	potato dumplings

Kartoffelknödel	potato dumplings
Kartoffeln	potatoes
Kartoffelpuffer	potato fritters
Kartoffelpüree	potato purée
Kartoffelsalat	potato salad
Kartoffelsuppe	potato soup
Käse	cheese
Käse-Sahne-Torte	cream cheesecake
Käsegebäck	cheese savouries
Käsekuchen	cheesecake
Käseplatte	selection of cheeses
Käsesalat	cheese salad
Käsesoße	cheese sauce
Käsespätzle	home-made noodles with cheese
Kasseler Rippenspeer	salted rib of pork
Kasserolle	casserole
Kassler	smoked and braised pork chop
Kastanien	chestnuts
Katenrauchwurst	smoked sausage
Keule	leg, haunch
Kieler Sprotten	smoked sprats
Kirschen	cherries
klare Brühe	clear soup
Klößchensuppe	clear soup with dumplings
Klöße	dumplings
Knäckebrot	crispbread
Knacker	frankfurter(s)
Knackwurst	frankfurter
Knoblauch	garlic
Knoblauchbrot	garlic bread
Knochen	bone
Knochenschinken	ham on the bone
Knödel	dumplings
Kognak	brandy
Kohl	cabbage
Kohl und Pinkel	cabbage, potatoes, sausage and smoked meat
Kohlrabi	kohlrabi (type of cabbage)
Kohlrouladen	stuffed cabbage leaves
Kompott	stewed fruit
Konfitüre	jam

Königinpastete	chicken vol-au-vent
Königsberger Klopse	meatballs in caper sauce
Königskuchen	type of fruit cake
Kopfsalat	lettuce
Kotelett	chop
Krabben	shrimps; prawns
Krabbencocktail	prawn cocktail
Kraftbrühe	beef consommé
Kräuter	herbs
Kräuterbutter	herb butter
Kräuterkäse	cheese flavoured with herbs
Kräuterquark	curd cheese with herbs
Kräutersoße	herb sauce
Kräutertee	herbal tea
Krautsalat	coleslaw
Krautwickel	stuffed cabbage leaves
Krebs	crayfish
Kresse	cress
Kroketten	croquettes
Kruste	crust
Kuchen	cake
Kürbis	pumpkin
Labskaus	meat, fish and potato stew
Lachs	salmon
Lachsersatz	sliced and salted pollack (fish)
Lachsforelle	sea trout
Lachsschinken	smoked rolled fillet of ham
Lamm	lamb
Lammrücken	saddle of lamb
Langusten	crayfish
Lauch	leek
Leber	liver
Leberkäse	baked pork and beef loaf
Leberklöße	liver dumplings
Leberknödel	liver dumplings
Leberpastete	liver pâté
Leberwurst	liver pâté
Lebkuchen	type of gingerbread, often chocolate-covered
Leipziger Allerlei	mixed vegetables
Likör	liqueur

Limonade	lemonade
Linseneintopf	lentil stew
Linsensuppe	lentil soup
mager	lean
Majoran	marjoram
Makrele	mackerel
Makronen	macaroons
Mandeln	almonds
mariniert	marinaded, pickled
Markklößchen	marrow dumplings
Marmelade	jam
Marmorkuchen	marble cake
Maronen	sweet chestnuts
Matjes(hering)	young herring
Medaillons	small fillets
Meeresfische	seafish
Meeresfrüchte	seafood
Meerrettich	horseradish
Meerrettichsoße	horseradish sauce
Mehlspeise	sweet dish made with flour, milk, butter and eggs
Melone	melon
Miesmuscheln	mussels
Milch	milk
Milchmixgetränk	milk shake
Milchreis	rice pudding
Mineralwasser	(sparkling) mineral water
Mohnkuchen	poppyseed cake
Möhren	carrots
Mohrrüben	carrots
Most	fruit wine
Mus	purée
Muscheln	mussels
Muskat(nuß)	nutmeg
MWSt = Mehrwertsteuer	VAT
nach Art des Hauses	of the house
nach Hausfrauenart	home-made
Nachspeisen	desserts
Nachtisch	dessert
Napfkuchen	ring-shaped poundcake
natürlich	natural

Nieren	kidneys
Nudeln	pasta
Nudelsalat	noodle salad
Nudelsuppe	noodle soup
Nüsse	nuts
Obstsalat	fruit salad
Ochsenschwanzsuppe	oxtail soup
Öl	oil
Oliven	olives
Olivenöl	olive oil
Omelett	omelette
Orangen	oranges
Orangensaft	orange juice
Palatschinken	stuffed pancakes
paniert	with breadcrumbs
Paprika	peppers
Paprikasalat	pepper salad
Paprikaschoten	peppers
Paradiesäpfel	tomatoes
Parmesankäse	parmesan cheese
Pastete	vol-au-vent
Pellkartoffeln	potatoes boiled in their jackets
Petersilie	parsley
Petersilienkartoffeln	potatoes with parsley
Pfannkuchen	pancake(s)
Pfeffer	pepper
Pfifferlinge	chanterelles
Pfirsiche	peaches
Pflaumen	plums
Pflaumenkuchen	plum tart
Pflaumenmus	plum jam
Pichelsteiner Topf	vegetable stew with diced beef
pikant	spicy
Pikkolo	quarter bottle of champagne
Pilze	mushrooms
Pilzsoße	mushroom sauce
Pilzsuppe	mushroom soup
Platte	selection
pochiert	poached
Pökelfleisch	salt meat
Pommes frites	French fried potatoes

Porree	leek
Potthast	braised beef with sauce
Poularde	young chicken
Preiselbeeren	cranberries
Preßkopf	brawn
Prinzeßbohnen	unsliced runner beans
Pumpernickel	black rye bread
Püree	(potato) purée
püriert	puréed
Putenschenkel	turkey leg
Puter	turkey
Quark	curd cheese
Quarkspeise	curd cheese dish
Radieschen	radishes
Rahm	(sour) cream
Räucheraal	smoked eel
Räucherhering	kipper, smoked herring
Räucherlachs	smoked salmon
Räucherspeck	smoked bacon
Rauchfleisch	smoked meat
Rehbraten	roast venison
Rehgulasch	venison goulash
Rehkeule	haunch of venison
Rehrücken	saddle of venison
Reibekuchen	potato waffles
Reis	rice
Reisauflauf	rice pudding
Reisbrei	creamed rice
Reisrand	with rice
Reissalat	rice salad
Remoulade	remoulade – mayonnaise flavoured with herbs, mustard and capers
Renke	whitefish
Rettich	radish
Rhabarber	rhubarb
Rheinischer Sauerbraten	braised beef
Rinderbraten	pot roast
Rinderfilet	fillet steak
Rinderrouladen	stuffed beef rolls
Rinderzunge	ox tongue
Rindfleisch	beef

Rindfleischsalat	beef salad
Rindfleischsuppe	beef broth
Rippchen	spareribs
Risi-Pisi	rice and peas
Risotto	risotto
roh	raw
Rohkostplatte	selection of salads
Rollmops	rolled-up pickled herring, rollmops
rosa	rare to medium
Rosenkohl	Brussels sprouts
Rosinen	raisins
Rostbraten	roast
Rostbratwurst	barbecued sausage
Rösti	fried potatoes and onions
Röstkartoffeln	fried potatoes
Rotbarsch	type of perch
Rote Bete	beetroot
rote Grütze	red fruit jelly
Rotkohl	red cabbage
Rotkraut	red cabbage
Rotwein	red wine
Rührei mit Speck	scrambled egg with bacon
Rühreier	scrambled eggs
Rumpsteak	rump steak
Russische Eier	egg mayonnaise
Sahne	cream
Sahnesoße	cream sauce
Sahnetorte	cream gâteau
Salate	salads
Salatplatte	selection of salads
Salatsoße	salad dressing
Salz	salt
Salzburger Nockerln	sweet soufflés
Salzheringe	salted herrings
Salzkartoffeln	boiled potatoes
Salzkruste	salty crusted skin
Sandkuchen	type of Madeira cake
sauer	sour
Sauerbraten	marinaded pot roast
Sauerkraut	white cabbage, finely chopped and pickled
Sauerrahm	sour cream

Schaschlik	(shish-)kebab
Schattenmorellen	morello cherries
Schellfisch	haddock
Schildkrötensuppe	real turtle soup
Schillerlocken	smoked haddock rolls
Schinken	ham
Schinkenröllchen	rolled ham
Schinkenwurst	ham sausage
Schlachtplatte	selection of fresh sausages
Schlagsahne	whipped cream
Schlei	tench
Schmorbraten	pot roast
Schnecken	snails
Schnittlauch	chives
Schnitzel	breaded cutlet
Schokolade	chocolate
Scholle	plaice
Schulterstück	slice of shoulder
Schwarzbrot	brown rye bread
Schwarzwälder Kirschtorte	Black Forest cherry gâteau
Schwarzwurzeln	salsifies
Schweinebauch	belly of pork
Schweinebraten	roast pork
Schweinefilet	fillet of pork
Schweinefleisch	pork
Schweinekotelett	pork chop
Schweineleber	pig's liver
Schweinerippe	cured pork chop
Schweinerollbraten	rolled roast of pork
Schweineschmorbraten	roast pork
Schweineschnitzel	pork fillet
Schweinshaxe	knuckle of pork
Seelachs	pollack (fish)
Seezunge	sole
Sekt	sparkling wine, champagne
Sellerie	celeriac
Selleriesalat	celeriac salad
Semmel	bread roll
Semmelknödel	bread dumplings
Senf	mustard
Senfsahnesoße	mustard and cream sauce

Senfsoße	mustard sauce
Serbisches Reisfleisch	diced pork, onions, tomatoes and rice
Soleier	pickled eggs
Soße	sauce, gravy
Soufflé	soufflé
Spanferkel	suckling pig
Spargel	asparagus
Spargelcremesuppe	cream of asparagus soup
Spätzle	home-made noodles
Speck	fatty bacon
Speckknödel	bacon dumplings
Specksoße	bacon sauce
Speisekarte	menu
Spezialität des Hauses	speciality
Spiegeleier	fried eggs
Spießbraten	joint roasted on a spit
Spinat	spinach
Spitzkohl	white cabbage
Sprotten	sprats
Sprudel(wasser)	mineral water
Stachelbeeren	gooseberries
Stangen(weiß)brot	French bread
Steak	steak
Steinbutt	turbot
Steinpilze	type of mushroom
Stollen	type of fruit loaf
Strammer Max	ham and fried egg on bread
Streuselkuchen	cake with crumble topping
Sülze	brawn
Suppen	soups
Suppengrün	mixed herbs and vegetables (used in soup)
süß	sweet
süß-sauer	sweet-and-sour
Süßspeisen	sweet dishes
Süßwasserfische	freshwater fish
Szegediner Gulasch	goulash with pickled cabbage
Tafelwasser	(still) mineral water
Tafelwein	table wine
Tagesgericht	dish of the day
Tageskarte	menu of the day
Tagessuppe	soup of the day

Tatar	steak tartare
Taube	pigeon
Tee	tea
Teigmantel	pastry case
Thunfisch	tuna
Tintenfisch	squid
Tomaten	tomatoes
Tomatensalat	tomato salad
Tomatensuppe	tomato soup
Törtchen	tart(s)
Torte	gâteau
Truthahn	turkey
überbacken	au gratin
Ungarischer Gulasch	Hungarian goulash
ungebraten	not fried
Vanille	vanilla
Vanillesoße	vanilla sauce
verlorene Eier	poached eggs
Vollkornbrot	dark whole grain bread
vom Grill	grilled
vom Kalb	veal
vom Rind	beef
vom Rost	grilled
vom Schwein	pork
Vorspeisen	hors d'oeuvres, starters
Waffeln	waffles
Waldorfsalat	salad with celery, apples and walnuts
Wasser	water
Wassermelone	watermelon
Weichkäse	soft cheese
Weinbergschnecken	snails
Weinbrand	brandy
Weincreme	pudding with wine
Weinschaumcreme	creamed pudding with wine
Weinsoße	wine sauce
Weintrauben	grapes
Weißbier	fizzy light-coloured beer made with wheat
Weißbrot	white bread
Weißkohl	white cabbage
Weißkraut	white cabbage
Weißwein	white wine

Weißwurst	veal sausage
Weizenbier	fizzy, light-coloured beer made with wheat
Wiener Schnitzel	veal in breadcrumbs
Wild	game
Wildschweinkeule	haunch of wild boar
Wildschweinsteak	wild boar steak
Windbeutel	cream puff
Wirsing	savoy cabbage
Wurst	sausage
Würstchen	frankfurter(s)
Wurstplatte	selection of sausages
Wurstsalat	sausage salad
Wurstsülze	sausage brawn
würzig	spicy
Zander	pike-perch, zander
Zigeunerschnitzel	veal with peppers and relishes
Zitrone	lemon
Zitronencreme	lemon cream
Zucchini	courgettes
Zucker	sugar
Zuckererbsen	mangetout
Zunge	tongue
Zungenragout	tongue ragoût
Zutaten	ingredients
Zwiebeln	onions
Zwiebelringe	onion rings
Zwiebelsuppe	onion soup
Zwiebeltorte	onion tart
Zwischengerichte	entrées

SHOPS AND SERVICES

This chapter covers all sorts of shopping needs and services, and to start with you'll find some general phrases which can be used in lots of different places, many of which are named in the list below. After the general phrases come some more specific requests and sentences to use when you've found what you need, be it food, clothing, repairs, film-developing, or a haircut. Don't forget to refer to the mini-dictionary for items you may be looking for.

Shops in Germany are generally open from 9 am to 6.30 pm, with some department stores and supermarkets staying open until 8.30 or 9 pm on Thursdays. On Saturdays, shops normally close at 2 pm, except for the first Saturday of each month, when most remain open until 6 pm.

Hairdressers are generally closed on Mondays.

USEFUL WORDS AND PHRASES

antique shop	der Antiquitätenladen	*antikvitayten-lahden*
audio equipment	die Phonoartikel	*fono-arteekel*
baker's	der Bäcker	*becker*
butcher's	der Metzger, der Fleischer	*metsger, flysher*
bookshop	die Buchhandlung	*bookHhantloong*
buy	kaufen	*kowfen*
cake shop	die Konditorei	*konditor-ry*
camera shop	der Fotoladen	*fotolahden*
camping equipment	die Campingartikel	*kempingarteekel*
carrier bag	die (Trage)tasche	*(trahguh-)tashuh*
cheap	billig	*billish*
china	das Porzellan	*portsellahn*
confectioner's	der Süßwarenladen	*soossvaren-lahden*
cost	kosten	*kosten*

craft shop	der Kunstgewerbeladen	*Koonstguverbe-lahden*
department store	das Kaufhaus	*kowfhowss*
dry cleaner's	die chemische Reinigung	*shaymishuh rynigoong*
electrical goods store	der Elektroladen	*elektrolahden*
expensive	teuer	*toyer*
fishmonger's	das Fischgeschäft	*fish-gusheft*
florist's	das Blumengeschäft	*bloomen-gusheft*
food store	das Lebensmittelgeschäft	*laybensmittel-gusheft*
fruit	das Obst	*ohpst*
gift shop	der Geschenkladen	*gushenk-lahden*
greengrocer's	die Gemüsehandlung	*gumoozuh-hantloong*
grocer's	das Lebensmittelgeschäft	*laybensmittel-gusheft*
hairdresser's	der Friseur	*frizur*
hardware shop	das Haushaltswarengeschäft	*howss-halts-varen-gusheft*
(for DIY etc)	die Eisenwarenhandlung	*ize-en-varen-hantloong*
hypermarket	der Großmarkt	*grohssmarkt*
jeweller's	der Juwelierladen	*yooveleer-lahden*
launderette	der Waschsalon	*vash-salong*
market	der Markt	*markt*
menswear	die Herrenbekleidung	*hairren-buklydoong*
newsagent's	der Zeitungsladen	*tsytoongs-lahden*
optician's	der Optiker	*optiker*
receipt	die Quittung	*kvittoong*
record shop	das Schallplattengeschäft	*shallplatten-gusheft*
sale	der Schlußverkauf	*shlooss-fairkowf*
shoe repairer's	der Schuhmacher	*shoomaKHer*
shoe shop	das Schuhgeschäft	*shoo-gusheft*
shop	der Laden	*lahden*

shop	das Geschäft	*gusheft*
souvenir shop	der Souvenirladen	*zooveneerlahden*
sports equipment	die Sportartikel	*shportarteekel*
sportswear	die Sportkleidung	*shport-klydoong*
stationer's	die Schreibwaren-handlung	*shryp-varen-hantloong*
supermarket	der Supermarkt	*zoopermarkt*
tailor	der Schneider	*shnyder*
till	die Kasse	*kassuh*
tobacconist's	der Tabakwarenladen	*tabakvaren-lahden*
toy shop	die Spielwaren-handlung	*shpeelvaren-hantloong*
travel agent's	das Reisebüro	*ryzuhbooro*
vegetables	das Gemüse	*gumoozuh*
wine merchant's	die Weinhandlung	*vine-hantloong*
women's wear	die Damen-bekleidung	*dahmen-buklydoong*

Excuse me, where is/are ...? *(in a supermarket)*
Entschuldigung, wo finde ich ...?
ent-shooldigoong vo finduh ish

Where is there a ... (shop)?
Wo gibt es ein Geschäft für ...?
vo geept ess ine gusheft foor

Where is the ... department?
Wo ist die ...-Abteilung?
vo ist dee ...-aptyloong

Where is the main shopping area?
Wo ist das Einkaufsviertel?
vo ist dass ine-kowfs-feertel

Is there a market here?
Gibt es hier einen Markt?
geept ess heer ine-en markt

I'd like ...
Ich hätte gern ...
ish hettuh gairn

Do you have ...?
Haben Sie ...?
hahben zee

How much is this?
Was kostet das?
vass kostet dass

Where do I pay?
Wo ist die Kasse?
vo ist dee kassuh

Do you take credit cards?
Akzeptieren Sie Kreditkarten?
aktsepteeren zee kredeetkarten

I think perhaps you've short-changed me
Könnte es sein, daß Sie mir zu wenig herausgegeben haben
kurntuh ess zine dass zee meer tsoo vaynish hairowss-gugayben hahben

Can I have a receipt?
Kann ich eine Quittung bekommen?
kan ish ine-uh kvittoong bukommen

Can I have a bag, please?
Haben Sie eine Tragetasche, bitte?
hahben zee ine-uh trahguh-tashuh bittuh

I'm just looking
Ich sehe mich nur um
ish zay-uh mish noor oom

I'll come back later
Ich komme später wieder
ish kommuh shpayter veeder

Do you have any more of these?
Haben Sie noch mehr davon?
hahben zee NOKH mair dafon

Do you have anything cheaper?
Haben Sie etwas Billigeres?
hahben zee etvass billigeress

Do you have anything larger/smaller?
Haben Sie etwas Größeres/Kleineres?
hahben zee etvass grursseress/kline-eress

Can I try it/them on?
Kann ich es/sie anprobieren?
kan ish ess/zee anprobeeren

Does it come in other colours?
Gibt es das auch in anderen Farben?
geept es dass OWKH in anderen farben

Could you gift-wrap it for me?
Könnten Sie es mir als Geschenk einpacken?
kurnten zee ess meer alss gushenk ine-packen

I'd like to exchange this, it's faulty
Ich möchte dies umtauschen, es ist defekt
ish murshtuh deess oomtowshen ess ist dayfekt

I'm afraid I don't have the receipt
Ich habe leider die Quittung nicht
ish hahbuh lyder dee kvittoong nisht

Can I have a refund?
Kann ich mein Geld zurückbekommen?
kan ish mine gelt tsoorook-bukommen

My camera isn't working
Meine Kamera funktioniert nicht
mine-uh kamera foonkts-yoneert nisht

I want a 36-exposure colour film, 100 ISO
Ich hätte gern einen Farbfilm für 36 Aufnahmen, 100 ISO
ish hettuh gairn ine-en farpfilm foor zex-oont-dryssish owfnahmen, hoondert ee-ess-oh

I'd like this film processed
Ich möchte diesen Film entwickeln lassen
ish murshtuh deezen film entvickeln lassen

Matt/glossy prints
Abzüge in matt/Hochglanz
aptsooguh in mat/hohKHglants

One-hour service, please
Ein-Stunden-Service, bitte
ine-shtoonden-'service' bittuh

Where can I get this mended?
Wo kann ich das reparieren lassen?
vo kan ish dass repareeren lassen

(clothes)
Wo kann ich das ausbessern lassen?
vo kan ish dass owssbessern lassen

Can you mend this?
Können Sie das reparieren?
kurnen zee dass repareeren?

(clothes)
Können Sie das ausbessern?
kurnen zee dass owssbessern

I'd like this skirt/these trousers dry-cleaned
Ich möchte diesen Rock/diese Hose reinigen lassen
ish murshtuh deezen rok/deezuh hohzuh rynigen lassen

When will it/will they be ready?
Wann ist es/sind sie fertig?
van ist ess/zint zee fairtish

I'd like some change for the washing machine/tumble dryer
Ich hätte gern Kleingeld für die Waschmaschine/den Trockner
ish hettuh gairn kline-gelt foor dee vash-masheenuh/dayn trockner

Can you help me work the machine, please?
Können Sie mir helfen, die Maschine zu bedienen?
kurnen zee meer helfen dee masheenuh tsoo budeenen

I'd like to make an appointment
Ich hätte gern einen Termin
ish hettuh gairn ine-en tairmeen

I want a cut and blow-dry
Schneiden und fönen, bitte
shnyden oont furnen bittuh

With conditioner
Mit Pflegespülung
mit pflayguh-shpooloong

No conditioner, thanks
Keine Pflegespülung, danke
kine-uh pflayguh-shpooloong dankuh

Just a trim, please
Nur etwas nachschneiden, bitte
noor etvass nahKH-shnyden bittuh

A bit more off here, please
Hier bitte etwas kürzer
heer bittuh etvass koortser

Not too much off!
Nicht zu kurz!
nisht tsoo koorts

When does the market open?
Wann macht der Markt auf?
van maKHt dair markt owf

Is there one today in a town nearby?
Gibt es heute einen in einer Stadt in der Nähe?
geept ess hoytuh ine-en in ine-er shtat in dair nay-uh

What's the price per kilo?
Was kostet es pro Kilo?
vass kostet ess pro keelo

Could you write that down, please?
Könnten Sie mir das bitte aufschreiben?
kurnten zee meer dass bittuh owfshryben

That's very expensive!
Das ist aber sehr teuer!
dass ist ahber zair toyer

That's fine. I'll take it
In Ordnung. Ich nehme es
in ortnoong ish naymuh ess

I'll have a piece of that cheese
Ich hätte gern ein Stück von dem Käse
ish hettuh gairn ine shtook fon daym kayzuh

About 250/500 grams
Etwa 250/500 Gramm
etva tsvy-hoondert-foonftsish/foonf-hoondert gram

A kilo/half a kilo of apples, please
Ein Kilo/Pfund Äpfel, bitte
ine keelo/pfoont epfel bittuh

A quarter of a kilo of ham, please
Ein halbes Pfund gekochten Schinken, bitte
ine halbess pfoont gukoKHten shinken bittuh

May I taste it?
Kann ich mal probieren?
kan ish mal probeeren

No, I don't like the taste
Nein, das schmeckt mir nicht so gut
nine dass shmekt meer nisht zo goot

That's very nice, I'll take some
Das ist sehr lecker, davon nehme ich etwas
dass ist zair lecker dahfon naymuh ish etvass

It isn't what I wanted
Es ist nicht das, was ich wollte
ess ist nisht dass vass ish volltuh

Things You'll See

Abteilung	department
Ausverkauf	sale
ausverkauft	sold out
Bäckerei	bakery
Blumen	flowers
Buchhandlung	bookshop
Büroartikel	office supplies
chemische Reinigung	dry cleaner's
Coiffeur	hairstylist
Damenkleidung	women's clothing
Damensalon	women's salon
Drogerie	chemist's
Fleischerei	butcher's
Friseur	barber's
Haarstudio	hairdressing studio
Heimwerkerbedarf	DIY supplies
herabgesetzt	reduced
Herrenkleidung	menswear
Herrensalon	men's hairdresser
Kasse	cash point
Kaufhaus	department store
Konditorei	cake shop

→

Lebensmittel	groceries
Metzgerei	butcher's
Mode	fashion
nicht berühren	do not touch
Obergeschoß	upper floor
Obst und Gemüse	fruit and vegetables
Pelze	furs
Preis	price
preiswert	bargain price, inexpensive
reduziert	reduced
Reisebüro	travel agent's
Schreibwaren	stationery
Schuhe	shoes
Schuhreparaturen	shoe repairs, heelbar
Selbstbedienung	self-service
Sommerschlußverkauf	summer sale
Sonderangebot	special offer
Sonderpreis	special price
Spielwaren	toys
Spirituosen	spirits
Spitzenqualität	high quality
Süßwaren	confectionery
Tabakwaren	tobacconist's
täglich frisch	fresh every day
Teppiche	carpets
Tiefgeschoß	lower floor, basement
Umtausch nur gegen Quittung	goods may not be exchanged without a receipt
vergriffen	unavailable, out of stock
vom Umtausch ausgeschlossen	may not be exchanged
Waschsalon	launderette
Winterschlußverkauf	winter sale
Zeitschriften	magazines
Zeitungen	newspapers

THINGS YOU'LL HEAR

Werden Sie schon bedient?
Are you being served?

Kann ich Ihnen helfen?
Can I help you?

Haben Sie es etwas kleiner?
Do you have anything smaller? (money)

Das haben wir gerade nicht vorrätig
I'm sorry we're out of stock

Das ist alles, was wir haben
This is all we have

Darf es sonst noch etwas sein?
Will there be anything else?

Darf es etwas mehr sein?
Is it okay if it's a bit over?

Wieviel hätten Sie gern?
How much would you like?

Wie möchten Sie es gern?
How would you like it?

Bezahlung mit Kreditkarte ist leider nicht möglich
I'm afraid it's not possible to pay by credit card

SPORT

Whatever your sport and wherever you are in Germany you will find no lack of facilities. The many lakes and rivers, as well as the North Sea and the Baltic Sea coasts, provide excellent opportunities for swimming, sailing, canoeing, fishing (permit required), sailboarding etc, while an extensive network of well-marked footpaths makes Germany an ideal country for walking. Cycling is popular too, and bikes can be hired almost everywhere, including at a large number of railway stations.

Germany is known throughout the world as a centre for winter sports, with around 300 resorts, mainly concentrated in the Alps, Black Forest and Harz. In addition, many other areas have good facilities for cross-country skiing, while most of the larger towns have an ice-rink, often open all year round.

Useful Words and Phrases

Alps	die Alpen	*alpen*
athletics	Leichtathletik	*lysht-atlaytik*
badminton	Badminton	*'badminton'*
ball	der Ball	*bal*
bicycle	das Fahrrad	*far-raht*
binding *(ski)*	die Bindung	*bindoong*
canoe	das Kanu	*kahnoo*
canoeing	Kanufahren	*kahnoofaren*
cross-country skiing	Langlauf	*langlowf*
current	die Strömung	*shtrurmoong*
cycle path	der Radweg	*rahtvayk*
cycling	Radfahren	*rahtfaren*
dive	tauchen	*towKHen*
diving board	das Sprungbrett	*shproongbret*
downhill skiing	Abfahrtslauf	*apfartslowf*
fishing	Angeln	*ang-eln*
fishing rod	die Angelrute	*ang-el-rootuh*
flippers	die Schwimmflossen	*shvimflossen*

football	Fußball	*foosbal*
football match	das Fußballspiel	*foosbal-shpeel*
game	das Spiel	*shpeel*
goggles	die Taucherbrille	*towKHerbrilluh*
golf	Golf	*golf*
golf course	der Golfplatz	*golfplats*
gymnastics	Gymnastik	*g[mnastik*
hike	wandern	*vandern*
hiking	Wandern	*vandern*
hang-gliding	Drachenfliegen	*drаKHenfleegen*
hillwalking	Bergwandern	*bairkvandern*
hockey	Hockey	*'hockey'*
hunting	die Jagd	*yahkt*
ice-hockey	Eishockey	*ice-'hockey'*
jogging	Jogging	*'jogging'*
mast	der Mast	*mast*
mountaineering	Bergsteigen	*bairk-shtygen*
nursery slope	der Idiotenhügel	*idee-ohten-hOOgel*
oars	die Ruder	*rOOder*
oxygen bottle	die Sauerstoffflasche	*zowershtoff-flashuh*
pedal boat	das Tretboot	*traytboht*
piste	die Piste	*pistuh*
racket	der Schläger	*shlayger*
ride *(verb)*	reiten	*rite-en*
riding	Reiten	*rite-en*
riding hat	die Reitermütze	*rite-er-mOOtsuh*
rock climbing	Felsklettern	*felz-klettern*
row *(verb)*	rudern	*rOOdern*
rowing boat	das Ruderboot	*rOOderboht*
run *(verb)*	laufen	*lowfen*
saddle	der Sattel	*zattel*
sail *(noun)*	das Segel	*zaygel*
(verb)	segeln	*zaygeln*
sailboard	das Windsurfbrett	*vintsurf-bret*
sailing	Segeln	*zaygeln*
go sailing	segeln gehen	*zaygeln gayen*

skate ***(verb)***	eislaufen	*ice-lowfen*
skates	die Schlittschuhe	*shlitt-shoo-uh*
skating rink	die Eislaufbahn	*ice-lowfbahn*
ski ***(noun)***	der Ski	*shee*
(verb)	Ski fahren	*shee faren*
ski boots	die Skistiefel	*shee-shteefel*
skiing	Skilaufen	*sheelowfen*
ski lift	der Skilift	*sheelift*
skin diving	Sporttauchen	*shport-towKHen*
ski pass	der Skipaß	*sheepas*
ski sticks	die Skistöcke	*shee-shturkuh*
ski tow	der Schlepplift	*shlep-lift*
ski trail	die Piste	*pistuh*
ski wax	das Skiwachs	*sheevax*
slalom	der Slalom	*slahlom*
sledge	der Schlitten	*shlitten*
snorkel	der Schnorchel	*shnorshel*
sports centre	das Sportzentrum	*shport-tsentroom*
stadium	das Stadion	*shtahdee-on*
surfboard	das Surfbrett	*surfbrett*
swim	schwimmen	*shvimmen*
swimming costume	der Badeanzug	*bahduh-antsook*
swimming pool	das Schwimmbad	*shvimbaht*
team	das Team	*'team'*
tennis	Tennis	*tennis*
tennis court	der Tennisplatz	*tennisplats*
tennis racket	der Tennisschläger	*tennis-shlayger*
toboggan	der Rodelschlitten	*rohdel-shlitten*
volleyball	Volleyball	*vollibal*
water-ski	Wasserski fahren	*vasser-shee faren*
water-skiing	Wasserski	*vasser-shee*
water-skis	die Wasserskier	*vasser-shee-er*
wet suit	der Tauchanzug	*towKHantsook*
go windsurfing	windsurfen gehen	*vintsurfen gayen*
winter sports	der Wintersport	*vintershport*
yacht	die Jacht	*yaKHt*

How do I get to the beach?
Wie komme ich zum Strand?
vee kommuh ish tsoom shtrant

How deep is the water here?
Wie tief ist das Wasser hier?
vee teef ist dass vasser heer

Is there an indoor/outdoor pool here?
Gibt es hier ein Hallenbad/Freibad?
geept ess heer ine hal-en-baht/frybaht

Is it safe to swim here?
Ist das Schwimmen hier sicher?
ist dass shvimmen heer zisher

Can I fish here?
Kann man hier angeln?
kan man heer ang-eln

Do I need a licence?
Braucht man eine Genehmigung?
browKHt man ine-uh gunaymigoong

Is there a golf course near here?
Gibt es in der Nähe einen Golfplatz?
geept ess in dair nay-uh ine-en golfplats

Do I have to be a member?
Muß man Mitglied sein?
mooss man mitgleet zine

I would like to hire a bicycle/some skis
Ich möchte ein Fahrrad/Skier leihen
ish murshtuh ine far-raht/shee-er ly-en

How much does it cost per hour/day?
Was kostet es pro Stunde/Tag?
vass kostet ess pro shtoonduh/tahk

I would like to take water-skiing lessons
Ich möchte gern Wasserskiunterricht nehmen
ish murshtuh gairn vassershee-oonterrisht naymen

Where can I hire ...?
Wo kann man ... leihen?
vo kan man ... ly-en

There's something wrong with this binding
Mit dieser Bindung stimmt etwas nicht
mit deezer bindoong shtimmt etvass nisht

How much is a weekly pass for the ski lift?
Was kostet ein Wochenpaß für den Skilift?
vass kostet ine vOKHen-pas foor dayn sheelift

What are the snow conditions like today?
Wie sind heute die Schneeverhältnisse?
vee zint hoytuh dee shnay-fairheltnissuh

I'd like to try cross-country skiing
Ich möchte gern Langlauf probieren
ish murshtuh gairn langlowf probeeren

I haven't played this before
Das habe ich noch nie gespielt
das hahbuh ish NOKH nee gushpeelt

Let's go skating/swimming
Sollen wir eislaufen/schwimmen gehen?
zollen veer ice-lowfen/shvimmen gayen

What's the score?
Wie steht's?
vee shtayts

Who won?
Wer hat gewonnen?
vair hat guvonnen

THINGS YOU'LL SEE

Angeln verboten	no fishing
Betreten der Eisfläche verboten	keep off the ice
Bootsverleih	boat hire
Eisstadion	ice rink
Fahrräder	bicycles
Fahrradverleih	bicycles for hire
Fahrradweg	cycle path
Freibad	open-air swimming pool
Gefahr	danger
gefährliche Strömung	dangerous current
Hafen	port
Hafenpolizei	harbour police
Hallenbad	indoor swimming pool
Karten	tickets
Lawinengefahr	danger of avalanches
Radweg	cycle path
Reitweg	bridle path
Rodelbahn	toboggan run
Schneeverwehung	snow drift
Schwimmen verboten	no swimming
Segelboote	sailing boats
Skipiste	ski slope
Sportzentrum	sports centre
Sprungschanze	ski jump
Stadion	stadium
Strand	beach
Tauchen verboten	no diving
Tauwetter	thaw
Umkleidekabine	changing rooms
Wanderweg	trail
Wassersport	water sports
zum Skilift	to the ski lift
zu verleihen	for hire

POST OFFICES AND BANKS

Post offices can be identified by a yellow sign with the word **Post(amt)** or the symbol of a post horn. Opening hours are usually from 9 am to 11.30 am or midday, and from 2 or 3 pm to 5.30 or 6 pm Monday to Friday, and 9 till 12 noon Saturday. Postboxes are yellow.

Most banks are open from 8.30 am or 9 am to 12.30 pm, and from 1.30 pm to 4 pm. On Thursdays they stay open until 6 pm. Banks are closed on Saturdays and Sundays. Foreign currency and traveller's cheques can also be exchanged at some of the larger hotels or at a bureau de change (**Wechselstube**). When changing money in a bank, it is customary to make your transaction at one desk and then go to a different desk, the cash desk, or **Kasse**, where your money will be paid out to you.

The German unit of currency is the common European currency, the **Euro** *(oyroh)*. One **Euro** is divided into 100 **Cent** *(tsent)*, and the coins come in 1, 2, 5, 10, 20 and 50 **Cent**; 1 and 2 **Euro**. Notes are available in 5, 10, 20, 50, 100, 200 and 500 **Euro**.

Credit cards are not that widely used in Germany, so don't be surprised if a shop or a railway station declines to accept payment by credit card.

Useful Words and Phrases

airmail	Luftpost	*looftposst*
bank	die Bank	*bank*
banknote	der Geldschein	*gelt-shine*
cash	das Bargeld	*bargelt*
cash dispenser	der Geldautomat	*gelt-owtomaht*
change	wechseln	*vexeln*
cheque	der Scheck	*shek*
chequebook	das Scheckbuch	*shekbOOKH*
collection	die Leerung	*layroong*

counter	der Schalter	*shalter*
credit card	die Kreditkarte	*kredeet-kartuh*
customs form	das Zollformular	*tsoll-formoolar*
delivery	die Zustellung	*tsoo-shtelloong*
deposit *(noun)*	die Einzahlung	*ine-tsahloong*
(verb)	einzahlen	*ine-tsahlen*
exchange rate	der Wechselkurs	*vexel-koors*
fax *(noun)*	das Fax	*fax*
(verb: document)	faxen	*faxen*
form	das Formular	*formoolar*
international money order	die Auslandsüberanweisung	*owss-lants-oober-anvyzoong*
letter	der Brief	*breef*
letter box	der Briefkasten	*breefkasten*
mail	die Post	*posst*
money order	die Postanweisung	*posst-anvyzoong*
package/parcel	das Paket	*pakayt*
post	die Post	*posst*
postage rates	das Porto	*porto*
postal order	die Geldanweisung	*gelt-anvyzoong*
postcard	die Ansichtskarte	*anzishts-kartuh*
postcode	die Postleitzahl	*posstlite-tsahl*
poste restante	postlagernde Sendungen	*posst-lahgernduh zendoong-en*
postman	der Briefträger	*breef-trayger*
post office	das Postamt	*posst-amt*
pound sterling	das englische Pfund	*eng-lishuh pfoont*
registered letter	das Einschreiben	*ine-shryben*
stamp	die Briefmarke	*breef-markuh*
surface mail	Post auf dem Landweg	*posst owf daym lantvayk*
traveller's cheque	der Reisescheck	*ryzuh-shek*
withdraw	abheben	*ap-hayben*
withdrawal	die Abhebung	*ap-hayboong*

How much is a letter/postcard to …?
Was ist das Porto für einen Brief/eine Postkarte nach …?
vass ist dass porto fOOr ine-en breef/ine-uh posstkartuh nahKH

I would like three 50 cent stamps
Ich hätte gern drei Briefmarken zu fünfzig Cent
ish hettuh gairn dry breef-marken tsoo fOOnftsish tsent

I want to register this letter
Ich möchte diesen Brief als Einschreiben senden
ish murshtuh deezen breef alss ine-shryben zenden

I want to send this parcel to …
Ich möchte dieses Paket nach … senden
ish murshtuh deezes pakayt nahKH … zenden

How long does the post to … take?
Wie lange ist die Post nach … unterwegs?
vee languh ist dee posst nahKH … oontervayks

Where can I post this?
Wo kann ich das aufgeben?
vo kan ish dass owfgayben

Is there any mail for me?
Ist Post für mich da?
ist posst fOOr mish da

I'd like to send a fax
Ich möchte ein Fax schicken
ish murshtuh ine fax shicken

This is to go airmail
Ich möchte das per Luftpost senden
ish murshtuh dass per looftposst zenden

I'd like to change this into euros
Ich möchte das gern in Euro wechseln
ish murshtuh dass gairn in oyroh vexeln

Can I cash these traveller's cheques?
Kann ich diese Reiseschecks einlösen?
kan ish deezuh ryzuh-sheks ine-lurzen

What is the exchange rate for the pound?
Wie steht der Kurs für das Pfund?
vee shtayt dair koors fōōr dass pfoont

Can I draw cash using this credit card?
Kann ich mit dieser Kreditkarte Geld abheben?
kan ish mit deezer kredeet-kartuh gelt ap-hayben

I'd like it in 20 euro notes
Ich möchte es gern in 20-Euro-Scheinen
ish murshtuh ess gairn in tsvantsish-oyroh-shine-en

Could you give me smaller notes?
Könnten Sie es mir in kleineren Scheinen geben?
kurnten zee ess meer in kline-eren shine-en gayben

Things You'll See

Absender	sender
ausfüllen	fill in
ausländische Währungen	foreign currency
Auslandsporto	overseas postage
Auszahlungen	withdrawals, cash desk
Brief	letter
Briefmarken	stamps
Bundespost	Federal Post Office
Drucksachen	printed matter
Einschreibsendungen	registered mail
Einzahlungen	deposits
Empfänger	addressee
Gebühren	charges
Geldautomat	cash dispenser
Geldwechsel	currency exchange

→

geöffnet	open
geschlossen	closed
Hausnummer	number
Inlandsporto	inland postage
Kasse	cash desk
Luftpostsendungen	airmail
nächste Leerung	next collection
Öffnungszeiten	opening hours
Ort	town, place
Päckchen	small parcels
Paket	parcels
Paketannahme	parcels counter
Porto	postage
Postamt	post office
Postanweisungen	money orders
Postkarte	postcard
postlagernde Sendungen	poste restante
Postleitzahl	postcode
Postsparkasse	giro bank
Postwertzeichen in kleinen Mengen	stamps in small quantities
Schalter	counter
Sparkasse	savings bank
Telefonzelle	telephone box
Wechselkurs	exchange rate
Wechselstube	bureau de change

You May Hear

Sie bekommen Ihr Geld an der Kasse
You'll get your money at the cash desk

COMMUNICATIONS

Telephones: Telephone boxes in Germany are yellow. International calls can only be made from boxes that show a green disc with the word **Ausland** or **International**. To phone the UK, dial 0044 followed by the area code (but omit the 0 which prefixes all UK area codes) and the number you want. Phonecards can be bought from post offices.

The tones you'll hear when telephoning in Germany are:

Dialling tone:	same as in UK
Ringing:	long high-pitched tone
Engaged:	rapid pips similar to UK
Unobtainable:	voice says **Kein Anschluß unter dieser Nummer**, and you'll hear three short pips of ascending pitch.

In German, telephone numbers are read out in pairs of numbers. For example, 302106 is said **dreißig, einundzwanzig, null sechs** ('thirty, twenty-one, zero six'). It will, of course, also be perfectly comprehensible to say a number as individual digits.

USEFUL WORDS AND PHRASES

call *(noun)*	der Anruf	*anroof*
(verb)	anrufen	*anroofen*
cardphone	das Kartentelefon	*karten-telefohn*
code	die Vorwahl	*forvahl*
crossed line	die Fehlverbindung	*fayl-fairbindoong*
dialling tone	das Amtszeichen	*amts-tsyshen*
email	die E-mail	*ee-mail*
email address	die E-mail Adresse	*ee-mail adressuh*
enquiries	die Auskunft	*owsskoonft*
extension	der Nebenanschluß	*nayben-anshlooss*
fax	das Fax	*fax*
internet	das Internet	*'internet'*

mobile phone	das Mobiltelefon	*mohbeeltelefohn*
modem	das Modem	*mohdem*
payphone	das Münztelefon	*moonts-telefohn*
phonecard	die Telefonkarte	*telefohn-kartuh*
reverse charge call	das R-Gespräch	*air-gushpraysh*
telephone	das Telefon	*telefohn*
telephone directory	das Telefonbuch	*telefohn-BOOKH*
Web site	die Webseite	*'website'*
wrong number	die falsche Nummer	*falshuh noommer*

Where is the nearest phone box?
Wo ist die nächste Telefonzelle?
vo ist dee naykstuh telefohn-tselluh

I would like the directory for ...
Ich hätte gern das Telefonbuch für ...
ish hettuh gairn dass telefohn-BOOKH foor

Can I call abroad from here?
Kann man von hier ins Ausland anrufen?
kan man fon heer inss owsslant anroofen

I would like to reverse the charges
Ich möchte ein R-Gespräch führen
ish murshtuh ine air-gushpraysh fooren

I would like a number in ...
Ich hätte gern eine Nummer in ...
ish hettuh gairn ine-uh noommer in

Could you give me an outside line?
Geben Sie mir bitte das Amt
gayben zee meer bittuh dass amt

How do I get an outside line?
Wie kann ich nach draußen telefonieren?
vee kan ish nahKH drowssen telefoneeren

Hello, this is … speaking
Hallo, hier spricht …
hallo heer shprisht

Is that …?
Ist das …?
ist dass

Speaking
Am Apparat
am aparaht

I would like to speak to …
Kann ich bitte … sprechen?
kan ish bittuh … shpreshen

Extension …, please
Anschluß …, bitte
anshlooss … bittuh

Please tell him/her … called
Bitte sagen Sie ihm/ihr, daß … angerufen hat
bittuh zahgen zee eem/eer dass … anguroofen hat

Would you ask him/her to call me back, please
Sagen Sie ihm/ihr bitte, er/sie möchte mich zurückrufen
zahgen zee eem/eer bittuh air/zee murshtuh mish tsoorook-roofen

Do you know where he/she is?
Wissen Sie, wo er/sie ist?
vissen zee vo air/zee ist

When will he/she be back?
Wann wird er/sie zurück sein?
van veert air/zee tsoorook zine

Could you leave him/her a message?
Können Sie ihm/ihr etwas ausrichten?
kurnen zee eem/eer etvass owssrishten

I'll ring back later
Ich rufe später zurück
ish roofuh shpayter tsoorook

Sorry, (I've got the) wrong number
Tut mir leid, ich habe mich verwählt
toot meer lite ish hahbuh mish fairvaylt

What's your fax number/email address?
Wie ist ihre Faxnummer/E-mail Adresse?
vee isst eeruh faxnummer/ee-mail adressuh

Did you get my fax/email?
Haben Sie mein Fax/meine E-mail erhalten?
hahben zee mine fax/mine-nuh ee-mail airhalten

Can I send an email/fax from here?
Kann ich von hier eine E-mail/ein Fax senden?
kan ish von hear ine-nuh ee-mail/ine fax senden

Please resend your fax
Bitte senden Sie Ihr Fax noch einmal
bittuh zenden zee ear fax NOKH ine-mahl

The Alphabet

a	*ah*	**h**	*hah*	**o**	*o*	**v**	*fow*
b	*bay*	**i**	*ee*	**p**	*pay*	**w**	*vay*
c	*tsay*	**j**	*yot*	**q**	*koo*	**x**	*ix*
d	*day*	**k**	*kah*	**r**	*air*	**y**	*oopsilon*
e	*ay*	**l**	*el*	**s**	*ess*	**z**	*tset*
f	*ef*	**m**	*em*	**t**	*tay*		
g	*gay*	**n**	*en*	**u**	*oo*		

Special German Characters

ä	*eh*	**ö**	*ur*	**ü**	*oo*	**ß**	*ess-tset*

Things You'll See

abnehmen	lift (the receiver)
Auskunft	(directory) enquiries
Auslandsgespräche	international calls
außer Betrieb	out of order
besetzt	engaged
defekt	out of order
Durchwahl	direct dialling
Einheit	unit
E-mail Adresse	email address
fasse dich kurz!	be brief!
Ferngespräche	long-distance calls
Fernsprecher	telephone
Feuer	fire
Feuerwehr	fire brigade
Gabel	hook
Gelbe Seiten	Yellow Pages
Geld einwerfen	insert money
Gespräch	call, conversation
Großbritannien	Great Britain
Hörer	receiver
Internet	internet
Karte ganz einschieben	push card right in
Münzen	coins
Notruf	emergency call
Ortsgespräche	local calls
Rufnummer	number
Störungsstelle	faults service
Telefonzelle	telephone box
Vereinigtes Königreich	United Kingdom
Vermittlung	operator
Vorwahl	code
wählen	to dial
warten	to wait
Webseite	Web site

THINGS YOU'LL HEAR

Am Apparat
Speaking

Wen möchten Sie sprechen?
Who would you like to speak to?

Sie sind falsch verbunden
You've got the wrong number

Wer spricht bitte?
Who's speaking?

Welche Nummer haben Sie?
What is your number?

Tut mir leid, er ist nicht im Hause
Sorry, he's not here

Er ist um drei Uhr zurück
He'll be back at three o'clock

Bitte rufen Sie morgen nochmal an
Please call again tomorrow

Ich werde ihm/ihr sagen, daß Sie angerufen haben
I'll tell him/her you called

Kein Anschluß unter dieser Nummer
Number unobtainable

Ich verbinde
I'll put you through

Bitte warten
Please hold

EMERGENCIES

In an emergency dial 110 for police or ambulance and 112 for fire. Drivers can get assistance from the **ADAC**, the German motoring organisation. If you break down on an autobahn, look for a small arrow on the marker posts at the side of the road: the arrow points in the direction of the nearest emergency telephone. Ask for the **Straßenwacht** (*shtrahssen-vaKHt*). Assistance will be free, but you will have to pay for parts.

Useful Words and Phrases

accident	der Unfall	*oonfal*
ambulance	der Krankenwagen	*kranken-vahgen*
assault (*verb*)	überfallen	*ωberfal-en*
breakdown	die Panne	*pannuh*
break down	eine Panne haben	*ine-uh pannuh hahben*
breakdown recovery	der Abschleppdienst	*ap-shlep-deenst*
burglar	der Einbrecher	*ine-breKHer*
burglary	der Einbruch	*ine-brooKH*
casualty department	die Unfallstation	*oonfal-stats-yohn*
crash	der Zusammenstoß	*tsoozammen-shtohss*
emergency	der Notfall	*nohtfal*
fire	das Feuer	*foyer*
fire brigade	die Feuerwehr	*foyer-vayr*
flood	die Überschwemmung	*ωbershvemmoong*
injured	verletzt	*fairletst*
lose	verlieren	*fairleeren*
pickpocket	der Taschendieb	*tashendeep*
police	die Polizei	*poli-tsy*
police station	die Polizeiwache	*poli-tsy-vaKHuh*
rob	rauben	*rowben*

steal	stehlen	*shtaylen*
theft	der Diebstahl	*deep-shtahl*
thief	der Dieb	*deep*
tow	abschleppen	*ap-shleppen*

Help!
Hilfe!
hilfuh

Look out!
Passen Sie auf!
pas-en zee owf

Stop!
Halt!
halt

This is an emergency!
Dies ist ein Notfall!
deess ist ine nohtfal

Get an ambulance!
Rufen Sie einen Krankenwagen!
roofen zee ine-en kranken-vahgen

Hurry up!
Beeilen Sie sich!
buh-ile-en zee zish

Please send an ambulance to …
Bitte schicken Sie einen Krankenwagen zu …
bittuh shicken zee ine-en kranken-vahgen tsoo

Please come to …
Bitte kommen Sie zu …
bittuh kommen zee tsoo

My address is …
Meine Adresse ist …
mine-uh adressuh ist

We've had a break-in
Bei uns ist eingebrochen worden
by oonss ist ine-gubroKHen vorden

There's a fire at ...
Es brennt in ...
ess brennt in

Someone's been injured/knocked down
Jemand ist verletzt/überfahren worden
yaymant ist fairletst/ooberfahren vorden

He's passed out
Er ist ohnmächtig
air ist ohnmeshtish

My passport/car has been stolen
Mein Paß/Auto ist gestohlen worden
mine pas/owto ist gushtohlen vorden

I've lost my traveller's cheques/money
Ich habe meine Reiseschecks/mein Geld verloren
ish hahbuh mine-uh ryzuh-sheks/mine gelt fairloren

I want to report a stolen credit card
Ich möchte den Diebstahl einer Kreditkarte melden
ish murshtuh dayn deep-shtahl ine-er kredeet-kartuh melden

It was stolen from my room
Es wurde aus meinem Zimmer gestohlen
ess voorduh owss mine-em tsimmer gushtohlen

I lost it in the park/on the train
Ich habe es im Park/im Zug verloren
ish hahbuh ess im park/im tsook fairlohren

My luggage has gone missing
Mein Gepäck ist verloren gegangen
mine gupek ist fairlohren gugang-en

Has my luggage turned up yet?
Ist mein Gepäck inzwischen aufgetaucht?
ist mine gupek intsvishen owfgutowKHt

The registration number is …
Mein amtliches Kennzeichen ist …
mine amtlishes ken-tsyshen ist

My car's been broken into
Mein Auto ist aufgebrochen worden
mine owto ist owfgubroKHen vorden

I've had a crash
Ich habe einen Unfall gehabt
ish hahbuh ine-en oonfal guhahpt

I've been mugged
Ich bin überfallen worden
ish bin œberfal-en vorden

My son's missing
Mein Sohn ist verschwunden
mine zohn ist fairshvoonden

He has fair/brown hair
Er hat helles/braunes Haar
air hat helless/browness har

He's … years old
Er ist … Jahre alt
air ist … yaruh alt

I've locked myself out
Ich habe mich ausgesperrt
ish hahbuh mish owss-gushpairt

He's drowning
Er ist am Ertrinken
air ist am airtrinken

She can't swim
Sie kann nicht schwimmen
zee kan nisht shvimmen

Things You'll See

Bergwacht	mountain rescue
Brand	fire
Erste Hilfe	first aid
Feuer	fire
Feuerlöscher	fire extinguisher
Krankenhaus	hospital
Lebensgefahr	danger of death
Nachtdienst	late night (chemist etc)
Notarzt	emergency doctor
Notausgang	emergency exit
Notfälle	emergencies
Notruf	emergency call
Notrufsäule	emergency telephone
Polizei	police
Polizeiwache	police station
Unfallrettung	ambulance, emergency service
Unfallstation	casualty department
Verkehrspolizei	traffic police

Things You'll Hear

Wo wohnen Sie?
What's your address?

Wo sind Sie?
Where are you?

Können Sie es/ihn beschreiben?
Can you describe it/him?

HEALTH

Under EC Social Security regulations visitors from the UK qualify for free medical treatment on the same basis as Germans themselves. If you want to make sure of being in possession of all necessary documentation, you should obtain a T4 from a main post office, fill in the attached E111 and get it stamped at the post office before travelling. With the E111, you'll also get a leaflet explaining how to obtain treatment.

In Germany, all chemists' shops are independent private concerns. There are no chainstore chemists like Boots in Britain. They sell medicines and a small assortment of goods which have some medicinal use. In every town you will find a chemist, or **Apotheke** (*apotaykuh*), that is open all night or over the weekend. Those that are closed will display a notice showing which one is open, and the local newspaper will also advertise the **dienstbereit** (*deenstburite*), or duty chemist. You may have to ring the night bell.

Useful Words and Phrases

ambulance	der Krankenwagen	*kranken-vahgen*
anaemic	blutarm	*blootarm*
appendicitis	die Blinddarm-entzündung	*blintdarm-ent-tsꝏndoong*
aspirin	die Kopfschmerz-tablette	*kopfshmairts-tablettuh*
asthma	das Asthma	*astma*
backache	die Rückenschmerzen	*rꝏken-shmairtsen*
bandage	der Verband	*fairbant*
bite *(by dog)*	der Biß	*biss*
(by insect)	der Stich	*shtish*
bladder	die Blase	*blahzuh*
blister	die Blase	*blahzuh*
blood	das Blut	*bloot*
blood donor	der Blutspender	*bloot-shpender*
burn	die Verbrennung	*fairbrennoong*

cancer	der Krebs	*krayps*
chemist	die Apotheke	*apotaykuh*
chest	die Brust	*broost*
chickenpox	die Windpocken	*vintpocken*
cold	die Erkältung	*airkeltoong*
concussion	die Gehirn-erschütterung	*guheern-airshꝏteroong*
constipation	die Verstopfung	*fairshtopfoong*
corn	das Hühnerauge	*hꝏner-owguh*
cough	der Husten	*hoosten*
cut	der Schnitt	*shnit*
dentist	der Zahnarzt	*tsahn-artst*
diabetes	die Zuckerkrankheit	*tsooker-krankhite*
diarrhoea	der Durchfall	*doorshfal*
dizzy	schwindlig	*shvintlish*
doctor	der Arzt	*artst*
earache	die Ohrenschmerzen	*oren-shmairtsen*
fever	das Fieber	*feeber*
filling	die Füllung	*fꝏlloong*
first aid	die Erste Hilfe	*airstuh hilfuh*
flu	die Grippe	*grippuh*
fracture	der Bruch	*brooKH*
German measles	die Röteln	*rurteln*
glasses	die Brille	*brilluh*
haemorrhage	die Blutung	*blootoong*
hay fever	der Heuschnupfen	*hoyshnoopfen*
headache	die Kopfschmerzen	*kopf-shmairtsen*
heart	das Herz	*hairts*
heart attack	der Herzinfarkt	*hairts-infarkt*
hospital	das Krankenhaus	*kranken-howss*
ill	krank	*krank*
indigestion	die Magen-verstimmung	*mahgen-fairshtimmoong*
injection	die Spritze	*shpritsuh*
itch	das Jucken	*yoocken*
kidney	die Niere	*neeruh*

lump	der Knoten	*k-nohten*
measles	die Masern	*mahzern*
migraine	die Migräne	*migraynuh*
mumps	der Mumps	*moomps*
nausea	die Übelkeit	*ꝏbelkite*
nurse *(female)*	die Kranken-schwester	*kranken-shvester*
(male)	der Krankenpfleger	*kranken-pflayger*
operation	die Operation	*operats-yohn*
pain	der Schmerz	*shmairts*
penicillin	das Penizillin	*penitsileen*
plaster *(sticky)*	das Pflaster	*pflaster*
plaster of Paris	der Gips	*gips*
pneumonia	die Lungen-entzündung	*loongen-entsꝏndoong*
pregnant	schwanger	*shvanger*
prescription	das Rezept	*retsept*
rheumatism	das Rheuma	*royma*
scald	die Verbrühung	*fairbrꝏ-oong*
scratch	der Kratzer	*kratser*
smallpox	die Pocken	*pocken*
sore throat	die Halsschmerzen	*halss-shmairtsen*
splinter	der Splitter	*shplitter*
sprain	die Verstauchung	*fairshtowKHoong*
sting	der Stich	*shtish*
stomach	der Magen, der Bauch	*mahgen, bowKH*
temperature	das Fieber	*feeber*
tonsils	die Mandeln	*mandeln*
toothache	die Zahnschmerzen	*tsahn-shmairtsen*
travel sickness	die Reisekrankheit	*ryzuh-krankhite*
ulcer	das Geschwür	*gushvꝏr*
vaccination	die Impfung	*impfoong*
vomit	erbrechen	*airbreshen*
whooping cough	der Keuchhusten	*koysh-hOOsten*
wound	die Wunde	*voonduh*

I have a pain in …
Ich habe Schmerzen in …
ish hahbuh shmairtsen in

I do not feel well
Ich fühle mich nicht wohl
ish fooluh mish nisht vohl

I feel sick
Mir ist schlecht
meer ist shlesht

I feel dizzy
Mir ist ganz schwindlig
meer ist gants shvindlish

It hurts here
Es tut hier weh
ess toot heer vay

It's a sharp/dull pain
Es ist ein stechender/dumpfer Schmerz
ess ist ine shteshender/doompfer shmairts

It hurts all the time
Es tut ständig weh
ess toot shtendish vay

It only hurts now and then
Es tut nur ab und zu weh
ess toot noor ap oont tsoo vay

It hurts when you touch it
Es tut weh, wenn man draufdrückt
ess toot vay ven man drowfdrookt

It hurts more at night
Nachts ist es schlimmer
naKHts ist ess shlimmer

It stings/it aches/it itches
Es brennt/es tut weh/es juckt
ess brennt/ess toot vay/ess yookt

I have a temperature
Ich habe Fieber
ish hahbuh feeber

I'm … months pregnant
Ich bin im … Monat schwanger
ish bin im … mohnat shvahngair

I need a prescription for …
Ich brauche ein Rezept für …
ish browKHuh ine retsept foor

I normally take …
Ich nehme normalerweise …
ish naymuh normahler-vyzuh

I'm allergic to …
Ich bin allergisch gegen …
ish bin alairgish gaygen

Can you take these if you're pregnant/breastfeeding?
Kann man diese während der Schwangerschaft/Stillzeit einnehmen?
kan man deezuh verent dair shvangershaft/shtiltsyte ine-naymen

Have you got anything for …?
Haben Sie etwas gegen …?
hahben zee etvass gaygen

I have lost a filling
Ich habe eine Füllung verloren
ish hahbuh ine-uh foolloong fairloren

Will he/she be all right?
Wird er/sie sich wieder erholen?
veert air/zee zish veeder erhohlen

Will he/she need an operation?
Muß er/sie operiert werden?
mooss air/zee opereert vairden

How is he/she?
Wie geht es ihm/ihr?
vee gayt ess eem/eer

THINGS YOU'LL SEE

Ambulanz	out-patients
Augenarzt	ophthalmologist, optician
Augenoptiker	optician
Bereitschaftsdienst	duty doctor/chemist
Blutdruck	blood pressure
dienstbereit	on duty
Facharzt für …	specialist for …
Frauenarzt	gynaecologist
Hals, Nasen, Ohren	ear, nose and throat
Inhalierer	inhaler
Intensivstation	intensive care unit
Krankenhaus	hospital
Krankenkasse	medical insurance
Krankenwagen	ambulance
Medikament	medicine
Notarzt	emergency doctor
Notaufnahme	casualty department
Notfälle	emergencies
Praktischer Arzt	General Practitioner
Sanitätsdienst	ambulance service
Sanitätsstelle	first-aid centre
Sprechstunde	surgery
Untersuchung	check-up
Termin	appointment
Wartezimmer	waiting room

Things You'll Hear

Nehmen Sie jeweils … Tabletten
Take … pills/tablets at a time

Mit Wasser
With water

Zum Zerkauen
Chew them

Einmal/zweimal/dreimal täglich
Once/twice/three times a day

Nur vor dem Schlafengehen
Only when you go to bed

Was nehmen Sie sonst?
What do you normally take?

Sie sollten besser zum Arzt gehen
I think you should see a doctor

Tut mir leid, das haben wir nicht
I'm sorry, we don't have that

Dafür brauchen Sie ein Rezept
For that you need a prescription

Auf nüchternen Magen
On an empty stomach

Der nächste bitte!
Next please!

CONVERSION TABLES

Distances

A mile is 1.6km. To convert kilometres to miles, divide the km by 8 and multiply by 5. Convert miles to km by dividing the miles by 5 and multiplying by 8.

miles	0.62	1.24	1.86	2.43	3.11	3.73	4.35	6.21
miles *or* km	**1**	**2**	**3**	**4**	**5**	**6**	**7**	**10**
km	1.61	3.22	4.83	6.44	8.05	9.66	11.27	16.10

Weights

The kilogram is equivalent to 2lb 3oz. To convert kg to lbs, divide by 5 and multiply by 11. One ounce is about 28 grams, and 8 ounces about 227 grams; 1lb is therefore about 454 grams.

lbs	2.20	4.41	6.61	8.82	11.02	13.23	19.84	22.04
lbs *or* kg	**1**	**2**	**3**	**4**	**5**	**6**	**9**	**10**
kg	0.45	0.91	1.36	1.81	2.27	2.72	4.08	4.53

Temperature

To convert Celsius degrees into Fahrenheit, the accurate method is to multiply the °C figure by 1.8 and add 32. Similarly, to convert °F to °C, subtract 32 from the °F figure and divide by 1.8.

°C	-10	0	5	10	20	30	36.9	40	100
°F	14	32	41	50	68	86	98.4	104	212

Liquids

A litre is about 1.75 pints; a gallon is roughly 4.5 litres.

gals	0.22	0.44	1.10	2.20	4.40	6.60	11.00
gals *or* litres	**1**	**2**	**5**	**10**	**20**	**30**	**50**
litres	4.54	9.10	22.73	45.46	90.92	136.40	227.30

Tyre Pressures

lb/sq in	18	20	22	24	26	28	30	33
kg/sq cm	1.3	1.4	1.5	1.7	1.8	2.0	2.1	2.3

MINI-DICTIONARY

The word for 'the' can be either **der**, **die** or **das**, depending on whether a noun is masculine, feminine or neuter. The plural is **die**. The corresponding words for 'a' are **ein**, **eine** or **ein**.

a ein, eine
about: about 16 etwa 16
accelerator das Gaspedal
accident der Unfall
accommodation die Unterkunft
ache der Schmerz
adaptor der Adapter
address die Adresse
adhesive der Klebstoff
admission charge der Eintrittspreise
after nach
aftershave das Rasierwasser
again nochmal
against gegen
agent der Vertreter
Aids Aids
air *(noun)* die Luft
air conditioning die Klimaanlage
aircraft das Flugzeug
airline die Fluglinie
airport der Flughafen
airport bus der Flughafenbus
aisle der Gang
alarm clock der Wecker
alcohol der Alkohol
all alle(s)
  all the streets alle Straßen
  that's all das ist alles
almost fast
alone allein
already schon
always immer
am: I am ich bin
ambulance der Krankenwagen
America Amerika
American *(man)* der Amerikaner
  (woman) die Amerikanerin
  (adj) amerikanisch
and und
ankle der Knöchel
another *(different)* ein anderer
  (one more) noch ein
  another room ein anderes Zimmer
  another coffee, please
  noch einen Kaffee, bitte
answering machine der Anrufbeanworter
antifreeze das Frostschutzmittel
antique shop das Antiquitätengeschäft
antiseptic das Antiseptikum
apartment die Wohnung
aperitif der Aperitif
appetite der Appetit
apple der Apfel
application form das Antragsformular
appointment der Termin
apricot die Aprikose
are: we/they are wir/sie sind
  you are Sie sind
  (sing, familiar) du bist
arm der Arm
art die Kunst
art gallery die Kunstgalerie
artist der Künstler
  (female) die Künstlerin
as: as soon as possible so bald wie möglich

ashtray der Aschenbecher
asleep: he's asleep er schläft
aspirin die Kopfschmerztablette
at: at the post office auf der Post
at the station am Bahnhof
at night in der Nacht
at 3 o'clock um 3 Uhr
attractive attraktiv
aunt die Tante
Australia Australien
Australian *(man)* der Australier
(woman) die Australierin
(adj) australisch
Austria Österreich
Austrian *(man)* der Österreicher
(woman) die Österreicherin
(adj) österreichisch
automatic automatisch
away: is it far away?
ist es weit von hier?
go away! gehen Sie weg!
awful furchtbar
axle die Achse

baby das Baby
baby wipes die Babytücher
back *(not front)* die Rückseite
(body) der Rücken
to come back zurückkommen
bacon der Speck
bacon and eggs Eier mit Speck
bad schlecht
bag die Tasche
baggage claim die Gepäckausgabe
bait der Köder
bake backen
baker der Bäcker
balcony der Balkon
ball der Ball
ball-point pen der Kugelschreiber
Baltic die Ostsee
banana die Banane
band *(musicians)* die Band
bandage der Verband
bank die Bank
banknote der (Geld)schein
bar *(drinks)* die Bar
bar of chocolate die Tafel Schokolade
barber's der Herrenfriseur
bargain das Sonderangebot
basement das Untergeschoß
basin *(sink)* das Becken
basket der Korb
bath das Bad
(tub) die Badewanne
to have a bath ein Bad nehmen
bathroom das Badezimmer
battery die Batterie
Bavaria Bayern
beach der Strand
beans die Bohnen
beard der Bart
beautiful schön
because weil
bed das Bett
bed linen die Bettwäsche
bedroom das Schlafzimmer
beef das Rindfleisch
beer das Bier
before ... vor ...
beginner der Anfänger
behind ... hinter ...
beige beige
Belgian *(man)* der Belgier
(woman) die Belgierin
(adj) belgisch
Belgium Belgien
bell *(church)* die Glocke
(door) die Klingel
below ... unter ...
belt der Gürtel
beside neben
best bester
better besser
between ... zwischen ...
bicycle das Fahrrad

big groß
bikini der Bikini
bill die Rechnung
bin liner die Mülltüte
bird der Vogel
birthday der Geburtstag
  happy birthday! viel Glück zum Geburtstag!
birthday card die Geburtstagskarte
birthday present das Geburtstagsgeschenk
biscuit das Plätzchen
bite *(noun: by dog)* der Biß
  (by insect) der Stich
  (verb) beißen
  (insect) stechen
bitter bitter
black schwarz
blackberry die Brombeere
blackcurrant die schwarze Johannisbeere
Black Forest der Schwarzwald
blanket die Decke
bleach *(noun)* das Bleichmittel
  (verb: hair) bleichen
blind *(cannot see)* blind
blinds die Jalousie
blister die Blase
blizzard der Schneesturm
blond *(adj)* blond
  (noun) die Blondine
blood das Blut
blouse die Bluse
blue blau
boat das Schiff
  (small) das Boot
body der Körper
  (corpse) die Leiche
boil *(verb)* kochen
boiler der Boiler
bolt *(noun: on door)* der Riegel
  (verb) verriegeln
bone der Knochen
bonnet *(car)* die Motorhaube
book *(noun)* das Buch
  (verb) buchen
bookshop die Buchhandlung
boot *(car)* der Kofferraum
  (footwear) der Stiefel
border die Grenze
boring langweilig
born: I was born in …
  ich bin in … geboren
both beide
  both of us wir beide
  both … and …
  sowohl … als auch …
bottle die Flasche
bottle opener der Flaschenöffner
bottom der Boden
  (part of body) der Hintern
  (sea) der Grund
bowl die Schüssel
box die Schachtel
box office die Kasse
boy der Junge
boyfriend der Freund
bra der Büstenhalter
bracelet das Armband
braces die Hosenträger
brake *(noun)* die Bremse
  (verb) bremsen
brandy der Weinbrand
bread das Brot
breakdown *(car)* die Panne
  (nervous) der Zusammenbruch
  I've had a breakdown
  ich habe eine Panne
breakfast das Frühstück
breathe atmen
bridge die Brücke
  (game) Bridge
briefcase die Aktentasche
Britain Großbritannien
British britisch
brochure die Broschüre

broken *(arm etc)* gebrochen
(vase etc) zerbrochen
(machine etc) kaputt
broken leg der Beinbruch
brooch die Brosche
brother der Bruder
brown braun
bruise der blaue Fleck
brush *(noun)* die Bürste
(paint) der Pinsel
(verb: hair) bürsten
(floor) kehren
Brussels Brüssel
bucket der Eimer
building das Gebäude
bumper die Stoßstange
burglar der Einbrecher
burn *(noun)* die Verbrennung
(verb) brennen
bus der Bus
business das Geschäft
it's none of your business
das geht Sie nichts an
bus station der Busbahnhof
busy *(occupied)* beschäftigt
(bar etc) voll
but aber
butcher's die Metzgerei
butter die Butter
button der Knopf
buy kaufen
by: by the window am Fenster
by Friday bis Freitag
by myself/himself allein

cabbage der Kohl
cable car die Drahtseilbahn
cable/satellite TV
das Kabel-/Satellitenfernsehen
café das Café
cagoule die Regenhaut®
cake der Kuchen
cake shop die Konditorei
calculator der Rechner
call: what's it called? wie heißt das?
camcorder der Camcorder
camera die Kamera
campsite der Campingplatz
camshaft die Nockenwelle
can *(tin)* die Dose
can I have ...? kann ich ... haben?
can you ...? können Sie ...?
Canada Kanada
Canadian *(man)* der Kanadier
(woman) die Kanadierin
(adj) kanadisch
canal der Kanal
candle die Kerze
canoe das Kanu
cap *(bottle)* der Verschluß
(hat) die Mütze
car das Auto
car seat *(for baby)* der Kindersitz
caravan der Wohnwagen
carburettor der Vergaser
card die Karte
cardigan die Strickjacke
careful sorgfältig
be careful! passen Sie auf!
caretaker der Hausmeister
carpet der Teppich
carriage *(train)* der Wagen
carrot die Möhre, die Karotte
case *(suitcase)* der Koffer
cash *(noun)* das Bargeld
(verb) einlösen
to pay cash bar bezahlen
cash dispenser der Geldautomat
cassette die Kassette
cassette player der Kassetten-recorder
castle das Schloß, die Burg
cat die Katze
cathedral der Dom
cauliflower der Blumenkohl
cave die Höhle
cemetery der Friedhof

central heating die Zentralheizung
centre *(middle)* die Mitte
certificate die Bescheinigung
chair der Stuhl
change *(noun: money)* das Kleingeld
(verb: money) wechseln
(clothes) sich umziehen
Channel der Kanal
Channel Tunnel der Kanaltunnel
cheap billig
check-in *(desk)* die Abfertigung
check in *(verb)* einchecken
cheers! prost!
cheese der Käse
chemist's die Apotheke
cheque der Scheck
chequebook das Scheckheft
cheque card die Scheckkarte
cherry die Kirsche
chess Schach
chest *(part of body)* die Brust
(furniture) die Truhe
chest of drawers die Kommode
chewing gum der Kaugummi
chicken das Huhn
(cooked) das Hähnchen
child das Kind
children die Kinder
china das Porzellan
chips die Pommes frites
chocolate die Schokolade
box of chocolates die Schachtel Pralinen
chop *(food)* das Kotelett
(verb: to cut) kleinschneiden
church die Kirche
cigar die Zigarre
(thin) das Zigarillo
cigarette die Zigarette
cinema das Kino
city die (Groß)stadt
city centre das Stadtzentrum
class die Klasse
classical music die klassische Musik
clean *(adj)* sauber
clear klar
clever klug
cling film die Folie
clock die Uhr
close *(near)* nah
(stuffy) stickig
(verb) schließen
closed geschlossen
clothes die Kleider
clubs *(cards)* Kreuz
clutch die Kupplung
coach der Bus
(train) der Wagen
coach station der Busbahnhof
coat der Mantel
coat hanger der (Kleider)bügel
cockroach die Küchenschabe
coffee der Kaffee
coin die Münze
cold *(illness)* die Erkältung
(adj) kalt
I have a cold ich bin erkältet
I am cold mir ist kalt
collar der Kragen
collection *(stamps etc)* die Sammlung
(postal) die Leerung
Cologne Köln
colour die Farbe
colour film der Farbfilm
comb *(noun)* der Kamm
come kommen
I come from ... ich komme aus ...
we came last week wir sind letzte Woche angekommen
come here! kommen Sie her!
compact disc die Compact-Disc
compartment das Abteil
complicated kompliziert
computer der Computer
concert das Konzert

conditioner *(hair)* die Haarspülung
condom das Kondom
conductor *(bus)* der Schaffner
(orchestra) der Dirigent
congratulations! herzlichen Glückwunsch!
consulate das Konsulat
contact lenses die Kontaktlinsen
contraceptive das Verhütungsmittel
cook *(noun)* der Koch
(verb) kochen
cooker der Herd
cooking utensils das Koch-geschirr
cool kühl
cork der Korken
corkscrew der Korkenzieher
corner die Ecke
corridor der Korridor
cosmetics die Kosmetika
cost *(verb)* kosten
what does it cost? was kostet das?
cotton die Baumwolle
cotton wool die Watte
cough *(noun)* der Husten
(verb) husten
country das Land
cousin *(male)* der Vetter
(female) die Kusine
crab die Krabbe
cramp der Krampf
crayfish der Krebs
cream *(for cake etc)* die Sahne
(lotion) die Creme
credit card die Kreditkarte
crisps die Chips
crowded überfüllt
cruise die Kreuzfahrt
crutches die Krücken
cry *(weep)* weinen
(shout) rufen
cucumber die Gurke
cufflinks die Manschettenknöpfe
cup die Tasse
cupboard der Schrank
curling tongs der Lockenstab
curls die Locken
curry das Curry
curtain der Vorhang
Customs der Zoll
cut *(noun)* der Schnitt
(verb) schneiden

dad der Vater
damp feucht
dance *(noun)* der Tanz
(verb) tanzen
Dane *(man)* der Däne
(woman) die Dänin
Danish dänisch
dangerous gefährlich
Danube die Donau
dark dunkel
daughter die Tochter
day der Tag
dead tot
deaf taub
dear *(person)* lieb
(expensive) teuer
deck chair der Liegestuhl
deep tief
delayed verspätet
deliberately absichtlich
Denmark Dänemark
dentist der Zahnarzt
dentures die Prothese
deny bestreiten
deodorant das Deodorant
department store das Kaufhaus
departure die Abfahrt
departure lounge die Abflughalle
develop *(film)* entwickeln
diamond *(jewel)* der Diamant
diamonds *(cards)* Karo
diarrhoea der Durchfall
diary das Tagebuch
dictionary das Wörterbuch

die sterben
diesel der Diesel
different verschieden
that's different! das ist etwas anderes!
I'd like a different kind ich möchte gern eine andere Sorte
difficult schwierig
dining room der Speiseraum
directory *(telephone)* das Telefonbuch
dirty schmutzig
disabled behindert
disposable nappies die Einwegwindeln
distributor *(car)* der Autohändler
dive *(noun)* der Sprung
(verb) tauchen
diving board das Sprungbett
divorced geschieden
do tun
how do you do? guten Tag
(on being introduced) freut mich
doctor der Arzt
document das Dokument
dog der Hund
doll die Puppe
dollar der Dollar
door die Tür
double room das Doppelzimmer
doughnut der Berliner
down herunter
(position) unten
down here hier unten
drawing pin die Heftzwecke
dress das Kleid
drink *(noun)* das Getränk
(verb) trinken
would you like a drink? möchten Sie etwas trinken?
drinking water das Trinkwasser
drive *(verb)* fahren
driver der Fahrer
driving licence der Führerschein
drunk betrunken
dry trocken
dry-cleaner's die (chemische) Reinigung
dummy *(for baby)* der Schnuller
during während
dustbin die Mülltonne
duster das Staubtuch
Dutch *(adj)* holländisch
Dutchman der Holländer
Dutchwoman die Holländerin
duty-free zollfrei
duvet die Steppdecke

each *(every)* jeder
five euros each fünf Euro das Stück
ear das Ohr
early früh
earrings die Ohrringe
ears die Ohren
east der Osten
easy leicht
eat essen
EC die EG
egg das Ei
either: either of them einer von beiden
either … or … entweder … oder …
elastic elastisch
elastic band das Gummiband
elbow der Ellbogen
electric elektrisch
electricity der Strom
else: something else etwas anderes
someone else jemand anders
somewhere else woanders
email die E-mail
email address die E-mail Adresse
embarrassing peinlich
embassy die Botschaft
embroidery die Stickerei
emerald der Smaragd
emergency der Notfall
emergency brake die Notbremse
emergency exit der Notausgang
empty leer
end das Ende

engaged *(couple)* verlobt
(occupied) besetzt
engine *(motor)* der Motor
England England
English *(adj)* englisch
(language) Englisch
Englishman der Engländer
Englishwoman die Engländerin
enlargement die Vergrößerung
enough genug
entertainment die Unterhaltung
entrance der Eingang
envelope der (Brief)umschlag
escalator die Rolltreppe
especially besonders
evening der Abend
every jeder
everyone jeder
everything alles
everywhere überall
example das Beispiel
for example zum Beispiel
excellent ausgezeichnet
excess baggage das Mehrgepäck
exchange *(verb)* (um)tauschen
exchange rate der Wechselkurs
excursion der Ausflug
excuse me! Entschuldigung!
exit der Ausgang
expensive teuer
extension lead die Verlängerungsschnur
eye das Auge
eyes die Augen

face das Gesicht
faint *(unclear)* blaß
(verb) ohnmächtig werden
fair *(funfair)* der Jahrmarkt
(just) gerecht, fair
false teeth die Prothese
family die Familie
fan *(ventilator)* der Ventilator
(enthusiast) der Fan
fan belt der Keilriemen
fantastic fantastisch
far weit
how far is it? wie weit ist es?
fare der Fahrpreis
farm der Bauernhof
farmer der Bauer
fashion die Mode
fast schnell
fat *(person)* dick
(on meat etc) das Fett
father der Vater
fax *(noun)* das Fax
(verb: document) faxen
fax machine das Faxgerät
feel *(touch)* fühlen
I feel hot mir ist heiß
I feel like ...
ich möchte gern ...
I don't feel well
mir ist nicht gut
feet die Füße
felt-tip pen der Filzstift
fence der Zaun
ferry die Fähre
fever das Fieber
fiancé der Verlobte
fiancée die Verlobte
field das Feld
fig die Feige
filling *(in tooth, cake)* die Füllung
(in sandwich) der Belag
film der Film
filter der Filter
filter papers das Filterpapier
finger der Finger
fire das Feuer
fire extinguisher der Feuerlöscher
fireworks das Feuerwerk
first erster
first aid die Erste Hilfe
first floor der erste Stock
first name der Vorname

fish der Fisch
fishing das Angeln
  to go fishing Angeln gehen
fishmonger's das Fischgeschäft
fizzy sprudelnd
flag die Fahne
flash *(camera)* der Blitz
flat *(level)* flach
  (apartment) die Wohnung
flavour der Geschmack
flea der Floh
flight der Flug
flippers die (Schwimm)flossen
floor *(ground)* der Boden
  (storey) der Stock
flour das Mehl
flower die Blume
flute die Flöte
fly *(insect)* die Fliege
  (verb) fliegen
fog der Nebel
folk music die Volksmusik
food das Essen
food poisoning die ebensmittelvergiftung
foot der Fuß
football der Fußball
for für
  for me für mich
  what for? wofür?
  for a week für eine Woche
foreigner der Ausländer
  (female) die Ausländerin
forest der Wald
forget vergessen
fork die Gabel
fortnight zwei Wochen
fourth vierter
France Frankreich
free frei
  (no charge) kostenlos
freezer der Gefrierschrank
French französisch
Frenchman der Franzose
Frenchwoman die Französin
fridge der Kühlschrank
friend der Freund
  (female) die Freundin
friendly freundlich
fringe *(hair)* der Pony
front: in front of ... vor ...
frost der Frost
fruit die Frucht
fruit juice der Fruchtsaft
fry braten
frying pan die (Brat)pfanne
full voll
  I'm full (up) ich bin satt
full board Vollpension
funny komisch
furniture die Möbel

garage die Garage
  (for repairs) die Werkstatt
garden der Garten
garlic der Knoblauch
gate das Tor
  (at airport) der Flugsteig
gay *(homosexual)* schwul
gear der Gang
gear lever der Schaltknüppel
gel *(hair)* das Gel
German *(man)* der Deutsche
  (woman) die Deutsche
  (adj) deutsch
  (language) Deutsch
Germany Deutschland
get *(fetch)* holen
  have you got ...? haben Sie ...?
  to get the train den Zug nehmen
get back: we get back tomorrow
  wir kommen morgen zurück
  to get something back
  etwas zurückbekommen
get in hereinkommen
  (arrive) ankommen
get off *(bus etc)* aussteigen

get on *(bus etc)* einsteigen
get out herauskommen
(bring out) herausholen
get up *(rise)* aufstehen
gift das Geschenk
gin der Gin
ginger *(spice)* der Ingwer
girl das Mädchen
girlfriend die Freundin
give geben
glad froh
glass das Glas
glasses die Brille
gloss prints die Glanzabzüge
gloves die Handschuhe
glue der Leim
go gehen
(travel) fahren
(by plane) fliegen
gold das Gold
good gut
goodbye auf Wiedersehen
government die Regierung
granddaughter die Enkelin
grandfather der Großvater
grandmother die Großmutter
grandparents die Großeltern
grandson der Enkel
grapes die Trauben
grass das Gras
great: great! prima!
Great Britain Großbritannien
green grün
grey grau
grill der Grill
grocer's das Lebensmittelgeschäft
ground floor das Erdgeschoß
groundsheet die Bodenplane
guarantee *(noun)* die Garantie
(verb) garantieren
guard der Wächter
guide der Führer
guide book der (Reise)führer
guitar die Gitarre
gun *(rifle)* das Gewehr
(pistol) die Pistole

hair das Haar
haircut der Haarschnitt
hairdresser's der Friseur
hair dryer der Fön
hair spray das Haarspray
half halb
half an hour
eine halbe Stunde
half board Halbpension
ham der gekochte Schinken
hamburger der Hamburger
hammer der Hammer
hand die Hand
handbag die Handtasche
handbrake die Handbremse
handle *(door)* die Klinke
handsome gutaussehend
hangover der Kater
happy glücklich
harbour der Hafen
hard hart
(difficult) schwer
hat der Hut
have haben
I have ... ich habe ...
have you got ...? haben Sie ...?
I have to go ich muß gehen
hay fever der Heuschnupfen
he er
head der Kopf
headache die Kopfschmerzen
headlights die Scheinwerfer
hear hören
hearing aid das Hörgerät
heart das Herz
hearts *(cards)* Herz
heater das Heizgerät
heating die Heizung
heavy schwer

heel *(shoe)* der Absatz
(foot) die Ferse
hello guten Tag
(on phone) hallo
help *(noun)* die Hilfe
(verb) helfen
hepatitis die Hepatitis
her: it's her sie ist es
it's for her es ist für sie
give it to her geben Sie es ihr
her book ihr Buch
her shoes ihre Schuhe
it's hers es gehört ihr
hi hallo
high hoch
highway code
die Straßenverkehrsordnung
hill der Berg
him: it's him er ist es
it's for him es ist für ihn
give it to him geben Sie es ihm
hire leihen, mieten
his: his book sein Buch
his shoes seine Schuhe
it's his es gehört ihm
history die Geschichte
hitchhike trampen
HIV positive HIV positiv
hobby das Hobby
Holland Holland
holiday der Urlaub
home: at home zu Hause
homeopathy die Homöopathie
honest ehrlich
honey der Honig
honeymoon die Hochzeitsreise
horn *(car)* die Hupe
(animal) das Horn
horrible schrecklich
hospital das Krankenhaus
hour die Stunde
house das Haus
how? wie?
hungry: I'm hungry ich habe Hunger
hurry: I'm in a hurry ich bin in Eile
husband der (Ehe)mann

I ich
ice das Eis
ice cream das Eis, die Eiscreme
ice lolly das Eis am Stiel
ice skates die Schlittschuhe
ice-skating: to go ice-skating
Schlittschuhlaufen gehen
if wenn
ignition die Zündung
ill krank
immediately sofort
impossible unmöglich
in in
in English auf Englisch
in the hotel im Hotel
indicator der Blinker
indigestion die Magenverstimmung
infection die Infektion
information die Information
injection die Spritze
injury die Verletzung
ink die Tinte
inn das Gasthaus
inner tube der Schlauch
insect das Insekt
insect repellent das Insektenmittel
insomnia die Schlaflosigkeit
instant coffee der Pulverkaffee
insurance die Versicherung
interesting interessant
internet das Internet
interpret dolmetschen
interpreter der Dolmetscher
(female) die Dolmetscherin
invitation die Einladung
Ireland Irland
Irish irisch
Irishman der Ire
Irishwoman die Irin

iron *(material)* das Eisen
(for clothes) das Bügeleisen
(verb) bügeln
is: he/she/it is … er/sie/es ist …
island die Insel
it es
Italian *(man)* der Italiener
(woman) die Italienerin
(adj) italienisch
Italy Italien
itch *(noun)* das Jucken

jacket die Jacke
jam die Marmelade
jazz der Jazz
jeans die Jeans
jellyfish die Qualle
jeweller's das Juweliergeschäft
jewellery der Schmuck
job die Arbeit
jog *(verb)* joggen
to go for a jog joggen gehen
joke der Witz
journey die Reise
jumper der Pullover
just *(only)* nur
it's just arrived es ist gerade angekommen

kettle der Wasserkessel
key der Schlüssel
kidney die Niere
kilo das Kilo
kilometre der Kilometer
kitchen die Küche
knee das Knie
knife das Messer
knit stricken
knitwear die Strickwaren
know wissen
(be acquainted with) kennen
I don't know ich weiß nicht

label das Etikett
lace die Spitze
laces *(shoe)* die Schnürsenkel
lady die Dame
lake der See
Lake Constance der Bodensee
lamb *(animal)* das Lamm
(meat) das Lammfleisch
lamp die Lampe
lampshade der Lampenschirm
land *(noun)* das Land
(verb) landen
language die Sprache
large groß
last *(final)* letzter
last week letzte Woche
at last! endlich!
late spät
the bus is late der Bus hat Verspätung
later später
laugh lachen
launderette der Waschsalon
laundry *(place)* die Wäscherei
(dirty clothes) die Wäsche
laxative das Abführmittel
lazy faul
leadfree bleifrei
leaf das Blatt
leaflet die Broschüre
learn lernen
leather das Leder
left *(not right)* links
there's nothing left
es ist nichts mehr übrig
left luggage locker
das Gepäck- schließfach
leg das Bein
lemon die Zitrone
lemonade die Limonade
length die Länge
lens die Linse
less weniger
lesson die Stunde

letter *(post)* der Brief
(alphabet) der Buchstabe
letter box der Briefkasten
lettuce der Kopfsalat
library die Bücherei
licence die Genehmigung
(driving) der Führerschein
life das Leben
lift *(in building)* der Fahrstuhl
could you give me a lift?
können Sie mich mitnehmen?
light *(noun)* das Licht
(adj: not heavy) leicht
(not dark) hell
light bulb die (Glüh)birne
lighter das Feuerzeug
lighter fuel das Feuerzeugbenzin
light meter der Belichtungsmesser
like: I like you ich mag Sie
I like swimming
ich schwimme gern
it's like ... es ist wie ...
like this so
lime *(fruit)* die Limone
lip salve der Lippen-Fettstift
lipstick der Lippenstift
liqueur der Likör
list die Liste
litre der Liter
litter der Abfall
little *(small)* klein
it's a little big es ist ein bißchen zu groß
just a little nur ein bißchen
liver die Leber
lobster der Hummer
lollipop der Lutscher
long lang
lorry der Lastwagen
lost property das Fundbüro
lot: a lot viel
loud laut
(colour) grell
lounge das Wohnzimmer
(in hotel) die Lounge
love *(noun)* die Liebe
(verb) lieben
lover *(man)* der Liebhaber
(woman) die Geliebte
low niedrig
(voice) tief
luck das Glück
good luck! viel Glück!
luggage das Gepäck
luggage rack die Gepäckablage
lunch das Mittagessen
Luxembourg Luxemburg

mad verrückt
magazine die Zeitschrift
mail die Post
make machen
make-up das Make-up
man der Mann
manager der Geschäftsführer
many: not many nicht viele
map *(of country)* die Landkarte
(of town) der Stadtplan
marble der Marmor
margarine die Margarine
market der Markt
marmalade die Orangenmarmelade
married verheiratet
mascara die Wimperntusche
mass *(church)* die Messe
match *(light)* das Streichholz
(sport) das Spiel
material *(cloth)* der Stoff
matter: it doesn't matter
das macht nichts
mattress die Matratze
maybe vielleicht
me: it's me ich bin's
it's for me es ist für mich
give it to me geben Sie es mir
meal das Essen

mean: what does this mean?
was bedeutet das?
meat das Fleisch
mechanic der Mechaniker
medicine die Medizin
meeting das Treffen
melon die Melone
men's toilets die Herrentoilette
menu die Speisekarte
message die Nachricht
midday der Mittag
middle: in the middle in der Mitte
midnight Mitternacht
milk die Milch
mine: it's mine es gehört mir
mineral water das Mineralwasser
minute die Minute
mirror der Spiegel
Miss Fräulein
mistake der Fehler
mobile phone das Mobiltelefon
modem das Modem
money das Geld
month der Monat
monument das Denkmal
moon der Mond
moped das Moped
more mehr
morning der Morgen
in the morning am Morgen
mother die Mutter
motorbike das Motorrad
motorboat das Motorboot
motorway die Autobahn
mountain der Berg
mountain bike das Mountain-Bike
mouse die Maus
mousse *(for hair)* der Schaumfestiger
moustache der Schnurrbart
mouth der Mund
move *(verb)* bewegen
(house) umziehen
don't move! stillhalten!
movie der Film
Mr Herr
Mrs Frau
Ms Frau
much viel
mum die Mutter
Munich München
museum das Museum
mushroom der Pilz
music die Musik
musical instrument das Musikinstrument
musician der Musiker
mussels die Muscheln
must: I must … ich muß …
mustard der Senf
my: my book mein Buch
my keys meine Schlüssel

nail *(metal, finger)* der Nagel
nail clippers der Nagelzwicker
nailfile die Nagelfeile
nail polish der Nagellack
name der Name
what's your name? wie heißen Sie?
nappy die Windel
narrow eng
near nah
near the door nahe der Tür
near London in der Nähe von London
necessary notwendig
neck der Hals
necklace die Halskette
need *(verb)* brauchen
I need … ich brauche …
there's no need das ist nicht nötig
needle die Nadel
negative *(photo)* das Negativ
neither: neither of them keiner von ihnen
neither … nor … weder … noch …
nephew der Neffe
Netherlands die Niederlande
never nie

new neu
news die Nachrichten
newsagent's der Zeitungsladen
newspaper die Zeitung
New Zealand Neuseeland
New Zealander
(man) der Neuseeländer
(woman) die Neuseeländerin
next nächster
next week nächste Woche
nice *(attractive)* hübsch
(pleasant) angenehm
(to eat) lecker
niece die Nichte
night die Nacht
nightclub der Nachtklub
nightdress das Nachthemd
night porter der Nachtportier
no *(response)* nein
I have no money ich habe kein Geld
noisy laut
north der Norden
Northern Ireland Nordirland
North Sea die Nordsee
nose die Nase
not nicht
notebook das Notizbuch
nothing nichts
novel der Roman
now jetzt
nowhere nirgendwo
nudist der Nudist
number die Zahl
(telephone) die Nummer
number plate das Nummernschild
nursery slope der Idiotenhügel
nut *(fruit)* die Nuß
(for bolt) die Mutter

occasionally gelegentlich
of von
the name of the hotel
der Name des Hotels
office das Büro
often oft
oil das Öl
ointment die Salbe
OK okay
old alt
how old are you? wie alt sind Sie?
olive die Olive
omelette das Omelette
on ... auf ...
one *(number)* eins
one beer/sausage ein Bier/eine Wurst
onion die Zwiebel
only nur
open *(verb)* öffnen
(adj) offen
operation die Operation
operator die Vermittlung
opposite: opposite the hotel
gegenüber dem Hotel
optician der Augenarzt
or oder
orange *(colour)* orange
(fruit) die Orange
orange juice der Orangensaft
orchestra das Orchester
ordinary gewöhnlich
other: the other ... der/die/das andere ...
our unser
it's ours es gehört uns
out aus
he's out er ist nicht da
outside außerhalb
oven der Backofen
over *(more than)* über
(finished) vorbei
(across) über
over there dort drüben
overtake überholen
oyster die Auster

pack of cards das Kartenspiel
package *(parcel)* das Paket

packet das Paket
(of cigarettes) die Schachtel
padlock das Vorhängeschloß
page die Seite
pain der Schmerz
paint *(noun)* die Farbe
pair das Paar
palace der Palast
pale blaß
pancake der Pfannkuchen
paper das Papier
(newspaper) die Zeitung
paracetamol die Schmerztablette
paraffin das Paraffin
parcel das Paket
pardon? bitte?
parents die Eltern
park *(noun)* der Park
(verb) parken
parsley die Petersilie
parting *(hair)* der Scheitel
party *(celebration)* die Party
(group) die Gruppe
(political) die Partei
passenger der Passagier
passport der Paß
pasta die Nudeln
path der Weg
pavement der Bürgersteig
pay bezahlen
peach der Pfirsich
peanuts die Erdnüsse
pear die Birne
pearl die Perle
peas die Erbsen
pedestrian der Fußgänger
peg *(clothes)* die Wäscheklammer
(tent) der Hering
pen der Stift
pencil der Bleistift
pencil sharpener der Bleistiftspitzer
penfriend der Brieffreund
(female) die Brieffreundin
penknife das Taschenmesser
people die Leute
pepper der Pfeffer
(red/green) der Paprika
peppermints die Pfefferminzbonbons
per: per night pro Nacht
perfect perfekt
perfume das Parfüm
perhaps vielleicht
perm die Dauerwelle
personal stereo der Walkman®
petrol das Benzin
petrol station die Tankstelle
phonecard die Telefonkarte
photograph *(noun)* das Foto
(verb) fotografieren
photographer der Fotograf
photocopier der Fotokopier
phrase book der Sprachführer
piano das Klavier
pickpocket der Taschendieb
picnic das Picknick
piece das Stück
pillow das Kopfkissen
pilot der Pilot
pin die Stecknadel
pineapple die Ananas
pink rosa
pipe *(for smoking)* die Pfeife
(for water) das Rohr
piston der Kolben
pizza die Pizza
place der Platz
(town etc) der Ort
at your place bei Ihnen
plant die Pflanze
plaster *(for cut)* das Pflaster
plastic das Plastik
plastic bag die Plastiktüte
plate der Teller
platform der Bahnsteig
play *(theatre)* das Stück
(verb) spielen

please bitte
plug *(electrical)* der Stecker
(sink) der Stöpsel
pocket die Tasche
poison das Gift
Poland Polen
Pole *(man)* der Pole
(woman) die Polin
Polish polnisch
police die Polizei
police officer der Polizist
police station das Polizeirevier
politics die Politik
poor arm
(bad quality) schlecht
pop music die Popmusik
pork das Schweinefleisch
port *(harbour)* der Hafen
(drink) der Portwein
porter *(hotel)* der Portier
possible möglich
post *(noun)* die Post
(verb) aufgeben
postbox der Briefkasten
postcard die Postkarte
poster das Poster
postman der Briefträger
post office das Postamt
potato die Kartoffel
poultry das Geflügel
pound *(money, weight)* das Pfund
powder das Pulver
(cosmetics) das Puder
pram der Kinderwagen
prawns die Krabben
prefer: I prefer ... ich mag lieber ...
prescription das Rezept
pretty *(beautiful)* schön
(quite) ziemlich
pretty good recht gut
priest der Geistliche
private privat
problem das Problem
public öffentlich
pull ziehen
puncture die Reifenpanne
purple lila
purse das Portemonnaie
push drücken
pushchair der Sportwagen
put legen, stellen, setzen
pyjamas der Schlafanzug

quality die Qualität
quarter das Viertel
quay der Kai
question die Frage
queue *(noun)* die Schlange
(verb) anstehen
quick schnell
quiet ruhig
quite *(fairly)* ziemlich
(fully) ganz

radiator der Heizkörper
(car) der Kühler
radio das Radio
radish der Rettich
(small red) das Radieschen
railway die Bahn
rain der Regen
raincoat der Regenmantel
raisins die Rosinen
rare *(uncommon)* selten
(steak) englisch
raspberries die Himbeeren
rat die Ratte
razor blades die Rasierklingen
read lesen
reading lamp die Leselampe
ready fertig
rear lights die Rücklichter
receipt die Quittung
receptionist die Empfangsperson
record *(music)* die Schallplatte
(sporting etc) der Rekord

record shop das Schallplattengeschäft
red rot
refreshments die Erfrischungen
relative der Verwandte
relax sich entspannen
religion die Religion
remember sich erinnern
I don't remember
ich erinnere mich nicht
rent *(verb)* mieten
reservation die Reservierung
rest *(noun: remainder)* der Rest
(verb: relax) sich ausruhen
restaurant das Restaurant
return *(come back)* zurückkommen
(give back) zurückgeben
return ticket die Rückfahrkarte
rice der Reis
rich reich
right *(correct)* richtig
(direction) rechts
ring *(to call)* anrufen
(wedding etc) der Ring
ripe reif
river der Fluß
road die Straße
rock *(stone)* der Stein
(music) der Rock
roll *(bread)* das Brötchen
roof das Dach
room das Zimmer
(space) der Raum
rope das Seil
rose die Rose
round *(circular)* rund
it's my round
das ist meine Runde
rowing boat das Ruderboot
rubber *(eraser)* der Radiergummi
(material) das Gummi
rubbish der Abfall
ruby *(stone)* der Rubin
rucksack der Rucksack
rug *(mat)* der Läufer
(blanket) die Wolldecke
ruins die Ruinen
ruler *(for drawing)* das Lineal
rum der Rum
run *(verb)* laufen
runway die Start- und Landebahn

sad traurig
safe sicher
safety pin die Sicherheitsnadel
sailing boat das Segelboot
salad der Salat
salami die Salami
sale *(at reduced prices)* der Schlußverkauf
salmon der Lachs
salt das Salz
same: the same dress
das gleiche Kleid
same again please
nochmal dasselbe, bitte
sand der Sand
sandals die Sandalen
sandwich das Butterbrot
sanitary towels die Damenbinden
sauce die Soße
saucepan der Kochtopf
sauna die Sauna
sausage die Wurst
say sagen
what did you say?
was haben Sie gesagt?
how do you say ...?
wie sagt man ...?
Scandinavia Skandinavien
scarf der Schal
(head) das Kopftuch
school die Schule
scissors die Schere
Scotland Schottland
Scotsman der Schotte
Scotswoman die Schottin
Scottish schottisch

screw die Schraube
screwdriver der Schraubenzieher
sea das Meer
seafood die Meeresfrüchte
seat der Sitz
seat belt der Sicherheitsgurt
second *(time)* die Sekunde
(in series) zweiter
see sehen
I can't see ich kann nichts sehen
I see ich verstehe
sell verkaufen
sellotape® der Tesafilm®
separate getrennt
separately getrennt
separated: we are separated wir leben getrennt
serious ernst
serviette die Serviette
several mehrere
sew nähen
shampoo das Shampoo
shave: to have a shave sich rasieren
shaving foam die Rasiercreme
shawl das Umhängetuch
she sie
sheet das (Bett)laken
shell die Muschel
shellfish *(as food)* die Meeresfrüchte
sherry der Sherry
ship das Schiff
shirt das Hemd
shoelaces die Schnürsenkel
shoe polish die Schuhcreme
shoes die Schuhe
shop das Geschäft
shopping das Einkaufen
(items bought) die Einkäufe
to go shopping einkaufen gehen
short kurz
shorts die Shorts
shoulder die Schulter
shower *(bath)* die Dusche
(rain) der Schauer
shower gel das Duschgel
shrimps die Garnelen
shutter *(camera)* der Verschluß
(window) der Fensterladen
sick *(ill)* krank
I feel sick mir ist übel
to be sick *(vomit)* sich übergeben
side die Seite
(edge) die Kante
sidelights das Standlicht
sights: the sights of ... die Sehenswürdigkeiten von ...
silk die Seide
silver *(colour)* silber
(metal) das Silber
simple einfach
sing singen
single *(one)* einziger
(unmarried) ledig, single
single room das Einzelzimmer
sister die Schwester
ski *(verb)* Ski fahren
ski binding die Skibindung
ski boots die Skistiefel
skid *(verb)* schleudern
skiing: to go skiing Skifahren gehen
ski lift der Skilift
skin cleanser der Hautreiniger
ski resort der Skiurlaubsort
skirt der Rock
skis die Skier
ski sticks die Skistöcke
sky der Himmel
sledge der Schlitten
sleep *(noun)* der Schlaf
(verb) schlafen
sleeping bag der Schlafsack
sleeping pill die Schlaftablette
slippers die Pantoffeln
slow langsam
small klein

smell *(noun)* der Geruch
(verb) riechen
smile *(noun)* das Lächeln
(verb) lächeln
smoke *(noun)* der Rauch
(verb) rauchen
snack der Imbiß
snow der Schnee
so so
not so much nicht so viel
soaking solution *(for contact lenses)* die Aufbewahrungslösung
soap die Seife
socks die Socken
soda water das Sodawasser
somebody jemand
somehow irgendwie
something etwas
sometimes manchmal
somewhere irgendwo
son der Sohn
song das Lied
sorry! *(apology)* Verzeihung!
I'm sorry es tut mir leid
sorry? *(pardon)* bitte?
soup die Suppe
south der Süden
South Africa Südafrika
souvenir das Souvenir
spa der Kurort
spade *(shovel)* der Spaten
spades *(cards)* Pik
spanner der Schraubenschlüssel
spares die Ersatzteile
spark(ing) plug die Zündkerze
speak sprechen
do you speak English? sprechen Sie Englisch?
I don't speak German ich spreche kein Deutsch
speed die Geschwindigkeit
spider die Spinne
spinach der Spinat
spoon der Löffel
sports centre das Sportzentrum
spring *(mechanical)* die Feder
(season) der Frühling
square *(shape)* das Quadrat
(in town) der Platz
stadium das Stadion
staircase die Treppe
stairs die Treppe
stamp die Briefmarke
stapler der Hefter
star der Stern
(film) der Star
start der Start, der Anfang
(verb) anfangen
station der Bahnhof
(tube) die Station
statue die Statue
steak das Steak
steal stehlen
it's been stolen es ist gestohlen worden
steamer *(boat)* der Dampfer
(cooking) der Dampfkochtopf
steering wheel das Lenkrad
sting *(noun)* der Stich
(verb) stechen
stockings die Strümpfe
stomach der Magen
stomachache die Magenschmerzen
stop *(bus stop)* die Haltestelle
(verb) anhalten
stop! halt!
storm der Sturm
strawberries die Erdbeeren
stream *(small river)* der Bach
street die Straße
string *(cord)* der Faden
(guitar etc) die Saite
strong *(person, drink)* stark
(material) stabil
(taste) streng
student der Student
(female) die Studentin

stupid dumm
suburbs der Stadtrand
sugar der Zucker
suit *(noun)* der Anzug
  it suits you es steht Ihnen
suitcase der Koffer
sun die Sonne
sunbathe sonnenbaden
sunburn der Sonnenbrand
sunglasses die Sonnenbrille
sunny: it's sunny es ist sonnig
sunshade der Sonnenschirm
suntan: to get a suntan braun werden
suntan lotion das Sonnenöl
suntanned braungebrannt
supermarket der Supermarkt
supper das Abendessen
supplement der Zuschlag
sure sicher
surname der Nachname
sweat *(noun)* der Schweiß
  (verb) schwitzen
sweatshirt das Sweatshirt
sweet *(not sour)* süß
  (candy) die Süßigkeit
swim *(verb)* schwimmen
swimming costume das Badekostüm
swimming pool das Schwimmbad
swimming trunks die Badehose
Swiss *(man)* der Schweizer
  (woman) die Schweizerin
  (adj) schweizerisch
switch der Schalter
Switzerland die Schweiz
synagogue die Synagoge

table der Tisch
tablet die Tablette
take nehmen
take-away der Schnellimbiß
take-off der Abflug
talcum powder das Körperpuder
talk *(noun)* das Gespräch
  (verb) reden
tall groß
tampons die Tampons
tangerine die Mandarine
tap der Hahn
tapestry der Wandteppich
tea der Tee
teacher der Lehrer
  (female) die Lehrerin
tea towel das Geschirrtuch
telephone *(noun)* das Telefon
  (verb) telefonieren
telephone box die Telefonzelle
television das Fernsehen
  to watch television fernsehen
temperature die Temperatur
  (fever) das Fieber
tent das Zelt
tent peg der Hering
tent pole die Zeltstange
than: bigger than größer als
thank *(verb)* danken
  thanks danke
  thank you danke schön
that: that man dieser Mann
  that woman diese Frau
  what's that? was ist das?
  I think that ... ich denke, daß ...
the der, die, das
  (pl) die
their: their room ihr Zimmer
  their books ihre Bücher
  it's theirs es gehört ihnen
them: it's them sie sind es
  it's for them es ist für sie
  give it to them geben Sie es ihnen
then dann
there da
  there is/are ... es gibt ...
  is/are there ...? gibt es ...?
these diese
they sie

thick dick
thin dünn
think denken
  I think so ich glaube ja
  I'll think about it ich überlege es mir
third dritter
thirsty durstig
  I'm thirsty ich habe Durst
this: this man dieser Mann
  this woman diese Frau
  what's this? was ist das?
  this is Mr … das ist Herr …
those diese da
  those things die Dinge dort
throat die Kehle
throat pastilles die Halstabletten
through durch
thunderstorm das Gewitter
ticket die Karte
tide: high tide die Flut
  low tide die Ebbe
tie *(noun)* die Krawatte
  (verb) festmachen
tight eng
tights die Strumpfhose
time die Zeit
  what's the time? wie spät ist es?
timetable *(train, bus)* der Fahrplan
tin die Dose
tin opener der Dosenöffner
tip *(money)* das Trinkgeld
  (end) die Spitze
tired müde
tissues die Taschentücher
to: to England nach England
  to the station zum Bahnhof
  to the doctor zum Arzt
toast der Toast
tobacco der Tabak
toboggan der Schlitten
today heute
together zusammen
toilet die Toilette
toilet paper das Toilettenpapier
tomato die Tomate
tomato juice der Tomatensaft
tomorrow morgen
tongue die Zunge
tonic das Tonic
tonight heute abend
too *(also)* auch
  (excessively) zu
tooth der Zahn
toothache die Zahnschmerzen
toothbrush die Zahnbürste
toothpaste die Zahnpasta
torch die Taschenlampe
tour die Rundreise
tour guide der Reiseleiter
  (female) die Reiseleiterin
tourist der Tourist
  (female) die Touristin
tourist office das Fremdenverkehrsbüro
towel das Handtuch
tower der Turm
town die Stadt
town hall das Rathaus
toy das Spielzeug
track suit der Trainingsanzug
tractor der Traktor
tradition die Tradition
traffic der Verkehr
traffic jam der Stau
traffic lights die Ampel
trailer der Anhänger
train der Zug
trainers die Turnschuhe
translate übersetzen
translator der Übersetzer
  (female) die Übersetzerin
travel agency das Reisebüro
traveller's cheque der Reisescheck
tray das Tablett
tree der Baum
trousers die Hose
true wahr

try versuchen
tunnel der Tunnel
Turk *(man)* der Türke
(woman) die Türkin
Turkey die Türkei
Turkish türkisch
tweezers die Pinzette
typewriter die Schreibmaschine
tyre der Reifen

umbrella der (Regen)schirm
uncle der Onkel
under ... unter ...
underground die U-Bahn
underpants die Unterhose
underskirt der Unterrock
understand verstehen
I don't understand ich verstehe nicht
underwear die Unterwäsche
university die Universität
unleaded bleifrei
until bis
unusual ungewöhnlich
up oben
(upwards) nach oben
up there da oben
urgent dringend
us: it's us wir sind es
it's for us es ist für uns
give it to us geben Sie es uns
use *(noun)* der Gebrauch
(verb) gebrauchen
it's no use es hat keinen Zweck
useful hilfreich
usual gewöhnlich
usually gewöhnlich

vacancy *(room)* ein freies Zimmer
vacuum cleaner der Staubsauger
valley das Tal
valve das Ventil
vanilla die Vanille
vase die Vase
veal das Kalbfleisch
vegetable das Gemüse
vegetarian der Vegetarier
(female) die Vegetarierin
(adj) vegetarisch
vehicle das Fahrzeug
very sehr
vest das (Unter)hemd
video *(tape, film)* das Video
video recorder der Videorecorder
video tape die Videocassette
Vienna Wien
view der Blick
viewfinder der Sucher
villa die Villa
village das Dorf
vinegar der Essig
violin die Violine
visit *(noun)* der Besuch
(verb) besuchen
visitor der Besucher
(female) die Besucherin
vitamin tablet die Vitamintablette
vodka der Wodka
voice die Stimme

wait warten
wait! warten Sie!
waiter der Ober
waiter! Herr Ober!
waiting room das Wartezimmer
(station) der Wartesaal
waitress die Kellnerin
waitress! Fräulein!
Wales Wales
walk *(noun: stroll)* der Spaziergang
(verb) gehen
to go for a walk spazieren gehen
wall *(inside)* die Wand
(outside) die Mauer
wallet die Brieftasche
war der Krieg
wardrobe der Kleiderschrank

warm warm
was: I was ich war
he/she/it was er/sie/es war
washing powder das Waschpulver
washing-up liquid das Spülmittel
wasp die Wespe
watch *(noun)* die (Armband)uhr
(verb) ansehen
water das Wasser
waterfall der Wasserfall
water heater das Heißwassergerät
wave *(noun)* die Welle
(verb: with hand) winken
wavy *(hair)* wellig
we wir
weather das Wetter
Web site die Webseite
wedding die Hochzeit
week die Woche
welcome willkommen
you're welcome keine Ursache
wellingtons die Gummistiefel
Welsh walisisch
Welshman der Waliser
Welshwoman die Waliserin
were: we/they were wir/sie waren
you were Sie waren
(sing, familiar) du warst
west der Westen
wet naß
what? was?
wheel das Rad
wheelchair der Rollstuhl
when? wann?
where? wo?
whether ob
which? welcher?
whisky der Whisky
white weiß
who? wer?
why? warum?
wide breit
wife die (Ehe)frau
wind der Wind
window das Fenster
wine der Wein
wing der Flügel
with mit
without ohne
woman die Frau
women's toilets die Damentoilette
wood *(material)* das Holz
wool die Wolle
word das Wort
work *(noun)* die Arbeit
(verb) arbeiten
(machine etc) funktionieren
worse schlechter
worst schlechtester
wrapping paper das Packpapier
(for presents) das Geschenkpapier
wrist das Handgelenk
writing paper das Schreibpapier
wrong falsch

year das Jahr
yellow gelb
yes ja
yesterday gestern
yet: is it ready yet?
ist es schon fertig?
not yet noch nicht
yoghurt der Joghurt
you Sie
(sing, familiar) du
for you für Sie/dich
with you mit Ihnen/dir
your Ihr
(sing, familiar) dein
your shoes Ihre/deine Schuhe
yours: is this yours? gehört das Ihnen?
(familiar) gehört das dir?
youth hostel die Jugendherberge

zip der Reißverschluß
zoo der Zoo